M000298439

The Speeches Of Ronald Reagan

Maureen Harrison & Steve Gilbert
Editors

□ 📖 Excellent Books □ 📖
www.excellentbooks.com

EXCELLENT BOOKS
www.excellentbooks.com

2nd Printing 2014.

Publisher's Cataloging in Publication Data

The Speeches of Ronald Reagan/
Maureen Harrison, Steve Gilbert, editors.
p. cm.
Bibliography: p.

1. Reagan, Ronald, 1911-2004. 2. United States—Presidents.
I. Harrison, Maureen. II. Gilbert, Steve.

E838.5 R.435 2004 973.227-DC21 LC 2004108966
ISBN 1-880780-26-7

Introduction

I do solemnly swear that I will faithfully execute the office of President of the United States, and will, to the best of my ability, preserve, protect, and defend the Constitution of the United States. So help me God.

—The Presidential Oath of Office

This anthology presents for readers and researchers alike edited excerpts from thirty-five extraordinary speeches by the late Ronald Reagan. From his first national political address, through the unforgettable speeches of his Presidency, and down to his farewell message, *The Speeches of Ronald Reagan* chronicles his thirty-year-long public conversation with the American people.

These speeches, taken one by one, represent one man's personal reactions to the triumphs and tragedies of his time in office. These same speeches, taken as a whole, constitute an oral history of that man's historic presidency.

We, the editors, have designed this book to easily acquaint readers, young and old alike, with the defining speeches of Reagan's political life. We have selected from eight years of almost daily speechmaking those words that made a difference. We have then carefully edited those words to present the essential short message within the much longer text. All of the speeches contained in this anthology are revealing of the man and his times. We hope that you find them interesting, thought-provoking, inspiring and informative.

On November 4, 1994 President Reagan, upon receiving a diagnosis of Alzheimer's Disease, issued a final message, "The Long Goodbye," to the American people. In it are sincere words befitting the measure of the man whose most important and enduring speeches you will find in this book: *Let me thank you, the American people, for giving me the great honor of allowing me to serve as your President.*

We hope that readers of this book find in its pages a true and lasting appreciation for the man as well as the President.

—M.H. & S.G.

Table of Speeches

Welcome Home!
45

You've come home to a people who for 444 days suffered the pain of your imprisonment, prayed for your safety, and most importantly, shared your determination that the spirit of free men and women is not a fit subject for barter.

—January 27, 1981

The Man With The Gun
47

Sick societies don't produce young men like [the Secret Service agent] who placed his body between mine and the man with the gun.

—April 28, 1981

This Last, Best Hope
48

Let us so conduct ourselves that two centuries from now, another Congress and another President, meeting in this Chamber as we are meeting, will speak of us with pride, saying that we met the test and preserved for them in their day the sacred flame of liberty—this last, best hope of man on Earth.

—January 26, 1982

The Sacred Fire Of Liberty
52

We live today in a time of climactic struggle for the human spirit, a time that will tell whether the great civilized ideas of individual liberty, representative government, and the rule of law under God will perish or endure.

—February 26, 1982

The Crusade For Freedom
54

Let us now begin … a crusade for freedom that will engage the faith and fortitude of the next generation. For the sake of peace and justice, let us move toward a world in which all people are at last free to determine their own destiny.

—June 8, 1982

A Noble Vision
60

We Americans have always been sustained, through good times and bad, by a noble vision—a vision not only of what the world around us is today but what we as a free people can make it be tomorrow.

—January 25, 1983

The Hope And Dream Of Freedom

64

The task that has fallen to us as Americans is to move the conscience of the world, to keep alive the hope and dream of freedom.

—February 18, 1983

The Evil Empire

66

Let us be aware that while they preach the supremacy of the state, declare its omnipotence over individual man, and predict its eventual domination of all peoples on the Earth, they are the focus of evil in the modern world.

—March 8, 1983

"Star Wars"

70

I call upon the scientific community in our country, those who gave us nuclear weapons, to turn their great talents now to the cause of mankind and world peace, to give us the means of rendering these nuclear weapons impotent and obsolete.

—March 23, 1983

The Beirut Bombing

73

I would like to ask you all—wherever you may be in this blessed land—to pray for these wounded young men and to pray for the bereaved families of those who gave their lives for our freedom.

—October 27, 1983

Freedom's Next Step

75

I've never felt more strongly that America's best days and democracy's best days lie ahead. We're a powerful force for good. With faith and courage, we can perform great deeds and take freedom's next step. And we will.

—January 25, 1984

Peace With Freedom

79

Our first responsibility is to keep America strong enough to remain free, secure, and at peace, and I intend to make sure that we do just that.

—March 2, 1984

Vietnam's Unknown Soldier
81

The Unknown Soldier who is returned to us today and whom we lay to rest is symbolic of all our missing sons, and we will present him with the Congressional Medal of Honor.

—May 28, 1984

The Fortieth Anniversary Of D-Day
84

We will always remember. We will always be proud. We will always be prepared, so we may always be free.

—June 6, 1984

This Springtime Of Hope
89

In this springtime of hope, some lights seem eternal; America's is.

—August 23, 1984

Second Inaugural Address
94

Let us remember that though our heritage is one of blood lines from every corner of the Earth, we are all Americans, pledged to carry on this last, best hope of man on Earth.

—January 21, 1985

A Second American Revolution
101

My fellow citizens, this nation is poised for greatness. The time has come to proceed toward a great new challenge—a second American Revolution of hope and opportunity.

—February 6, 1985

There's Work To Do!
105

If we move decisively, these years will not be just a passing era of good feeling, not just a few good years, but a true golden age of freedom. The moment is ours, and we must seize it. There's work to do!

—March 8, 1985

Terrorism
109

The American people are not—I repeat not—going to tolerate intimidation, terror, and outright acts of war against this nation and its people.

—July 8, 1985

The Challenger Disaster
114

We will never forget them, nor the last time we saw them, this morning, as they prepared for their journey and waved goodbye and "slipped the surly bonds of earth" to "touch the face of God."

—January 28, 1986

The American Dream
116

The American dream is a song of hope that rings through night winter air; vivid, tender music that warms our hearts when the least among us aspire to the greatest things.

—February 4, 1986

Just Say No!
120

Drug abuse is a repudiation of everything America is. The destructiveness and human wreckage mock our heritage.

—September 14, 1986

We The People
127

Wherever you are, America is depending on you to reach your highest and be your best because here in America, we the people are in charge.

—January 27, 1987

The Iran-Contra Controversy
133

A few months ago I told the American people I did not trade arms for hostages. My heart and my best intentions still tell me that's true, but the facts and the evidence tell me it is not.

—March 4, 1987

A Time For Choosing
October 27, 1964

In the last days of the 1964 election Ronald Reagan made this nationally televised speech in support of the Republican Party's Presidential candidate, Arizona Senator Barry Goldwater.

Thank you very much. Thank you and good evening. The sponsor has been identified, but unlike most television programs, the performer hasn't been provided with a script. As a matter of fact, I have been permitted to choose my own words and discuss my own ideas regarding the choice that we face in the next few weeks.

I have spent most of my life as a Democrat. I recently have seen fit to follow another course. I believe that the issues confronting us cross party lines. Now, one side in this campaign has been telling us that the issues of this election are the maintenance of peace and prosperity. The line has been used, "We've never had it so good."

But I have an uncomfortable feeling that this prosperity isn't something on which we can base our hopes for the future. No nation in history has ever survived a tax burden that reached a third of its national income.... We haven't balanced our budget 28 out of the last 34 years. We've raised our debt limit three times in the last twelve months, and now our national debt is one and a half times bigger than all the combined debts of all the nations of the world....

As for the peace that we would preserve, I wonder who among us would like to approach the wife or mother whose husband or son has died in South Vietnam and ask them if they think this is a peace that should be maintained indefinitely. Do they mean peace, or do they mean we just want to be left in peace? There can be no real peace while one American is dying some place in the world for the rest of us. We are at war with the most dangerous enemy that has ever faced mankind in his long climb from the swamp to the stars, and it's been said if we lose that war, and in so doing lose this way of freedom of ours, history will record with the greatest astonishment that those who had the most to lose did the least to prevent its happening. Well I think it's time we ask ourselves if we still know the freedoms that were intended for us by the Founding Fathers.

Not too long ago, two friends of mine were talking to a Cuban refugee, a businessman who had escaped from Castro, and in the midst of his story one of my friends turned to the other and said, "We don't know how lucky we are." And the Cuban stopped and said, "How lucky you are? I had someplace to escape to." And in that sentence he told us the entire story. If we lose freedom here, there's no place to escape to. This is the last stand on earth. And this idea that government is beholden to the people, that it has no other source of power except the sovereign people, is still the newest and the most unique idea in all the long history of man's relation to man. This is the issue of this election: Whether we believe in our capacity for self-government or whether we abandon the American revolution and confess that a little intellectual elite in a far-distant capitol can plan our lives for us better than we can plan them ourselves.

.... We have so many people who can't see a fat man standing beside a thin one without coming to the conclusion the fat man got that way by taking advantage of the thin one. So they are going to solve all the problems of human misery through government and government planning. Well, now, if government planning and welfare had the answer—and they've had almost 30 years of it—shouldn't we expect government to read the score to us once in a while? Shouldn't they be telling us about the decline each year in the number of people needing help? The reduction in the need for public housing?

But the reverse is true. Each year the need grows greater; the program grows greater. We were told four years ago that 17 million people went to bed hungry each night. Well that was probably true. They were all on a diet. But now we are told that 9.3 million families in this country are poverty-stricken on the basis of earning less than $3,000 a year. Welfare spending is 10 times greater than in the dark depths of the Depression. We are spending $45 billion on welfare. Now do a little arithmetic, and you will find that if we divided the $45 billion up equally among those 9 million poor families, we'd be able to give each family $4,600 a year. And this added to their present income should eliminate poverty. Direct aid to the poor, however, is only running only about $600 per family. It would seem that someplace there must be some overhead.

.... We are now going to solve the dropout problem, juvenile delinquency, by reinstituting something like the old CCC camps, and we are going to put our young people in these camps. But again we do some arithmetic, and we find that we are going to spend each year just on room and board for each young person we help $4,700 a year. We can send them to Harvard for $2,700! Don't get me wrong. I'm not suggesting Harvard is the answer to juvenile delinquency.

But seriously, what are we doing to those we seek to help? Not too long ago, a judge called me here in Los Angeles. He told me of a young woman who'd come before him for a divorce. She had six children, was pregnant with her seventh. Under his questioning, she revealed her husband was a laborer earning $250 a month. She wanted a divorce to get an $80 raise. She's eligible for $330 a month in the Aid to Dependent Children Program. She got the idea from two women in her neighborhood who'd already done that very thing.

Yet anytime you and I question the schemes of the do-gooders, we are denounced as being against their humanitarian goals. They say we are always "against" things, never "for" anything. Well, the trouble with our liberal friends is not that they are ignorant; it's just that they know so much that isn't so. We are for a provision that destitution should not follow unemployment by reason of old age, and to that end we've accepted Social Security as a step toward meeting the problem.

.... A young man, 21 years of age, working at an average salary—his Social Security contribution would, in the open market, buy him an insurance policy that would guarantee $220 a month at age 65. The government promises $127. He could live it up until he is 31 and then take out a policy that would pay more than Social Security. Now are we so lacking in business sense that we can't put this program on a sound basis, so that people who do require those payments will find they can get them when they are due, that the cupboard isn't bare? Barry Goldwater thinks we can.

At the same time, can't we introduce voluntary features that would permit a citizen who can do better on his own to be excused upon presentation of evidence that he had made provision for the non-earning years? Should we not allow a widow with children to work, and not lose the benefits supposedly paid for by her deceased husband? Shouldn't you and I be allowed to declare who our beneficiaries will be under this program, which we cannot do? I think we are for telling our senior citizens that no one in this country should be denied medical care because of a lack of funds....

In addition, was Barry Goldwater so irresponsible when he suggested that our government give up its program of deliberate, planned inflation, so that when you do get your Social Security pension, a dollar will buy a dollar's worth, and not 45 cents' worth?

I think we are for an international organization, where the nations of the world can seek peace. But I think we are against subordinating American interests to an organization that has become so structurally unsound that today you can muster a two-thirds vote on the floor of the General Assembly among nations that represent less than 10 percent of the world's population. I think we are against the hypocrisy of assailing our allies because here and there they cling to a colony, while we engage in a conspiracy of silence and never open our mouths about the millions of people enslaved in the Soviet colonies in the satellite nations.

.... No government ever voluntarily reduces itself in size. So governments' programs, once launched, never disappear. Actually, a government bureau is the nearest thing to eternal life we'll ever see on this earth. Federal employees number 2.5 million, and federal, state, and local, one out of six of the nation's work force employed by government. These proliferating bureaus with their thousands of regulations have cost us many of our constitutional safeguards. How many of us realize that today federal agents can invade a man's property without a warrant? They can impose a fine without a formal hearing, let alone a trial by jury? And they can seize and sell his property at auction to enforce the payment of that fine.... Last February 19 at the University of Minnesota, Norman Thomas, six-time candidate for President on the Socialist Party ticket, said, "If Barry Goldwater became President, he would stop the advance of socialism in the United States." I think that's exactly what he will do.

But as a former Democrat, I can tell you Norman Thomas isn't the only man who has drawn this parallel to socialism with the present administration, because back in 1936, Mr. Democrat himself, Al Smith, the great American, came before the American people and charged that the leadership of his Party was taking the Party of Jefferson, Jackson, and Cleveland down the road under the banners of Marx, Lenin, and Stalin. And he walked away from his Party, and he never returned till the day he died—because to this day, the leadership of that Party has been taking that Party, that honorable Party, down the road in the image of the labor Socialist Party of

England. Now it doesn't require expropriation or confiscation of private property or business to impose socialism on a people. What does it mean whether you hold the deed to the—or the title to your business or property if the government holds the power of life and death over that business or property? And such machinery already exists. The government can find some charge to bring against any concern it chooses to prosecute. Every businessman has his own tale of harassment. Somewhere a perversion has taken place. Our natural, unalienable rights are now considered to be a dispensation of government, and freedom has never been so fragile, so close to slipping from our grasp as it is at this moment. Our Democratic opponents seem unwilling to debate these issues. They want to make you and I believe that this is a contest between two men—that we are to choose just between two personalities.

Well, what of this man that they would destroy—and in destroying, they would destroy that which he represents, the ideas that you and I hold dear? Is he the brash and shallow and trigger-happy man they say he is? Well I've been privileged to know him "when." I knew him long before he ever dreamed of trying for high office, and I can tell you personally I've never known a man in my life I believed so incapable of doing a dishonest or dishonorable thing.

This is a man who in his own business, before he entered politics, instituted a profit-sharing plan before unions had ever thought of it. He put in health and medical insurance for all his employees. He took 50 percent of the profits before taxes and set up a retirement program, a pension plan for all his employees. He sent monthly checks for life to an employee who was ill and couldn't work. He provides nursing care for the children of mothers who work in the stores. When Mexico was ravaged by the floods in the Rio Grande, he climbed in his airplane and flew medicine and supplies down there.

An ex-GI told me how he met him. It was the week before Christmas during the Korean War, and he was at the Los Angeles airport trying to get a ride home to Arizona for Christmas, and he said that there were a lot of servicemen there and no seats available on the planes. And then a voice came over the loudspeaker and said, "Any men in uniform wanting a ride to Arizona, go to runway such-and-such," and they went down there, and there was a fellow named Barry Goldwater sitting in his plane. Every day in those weeks before

Christmas, all day long, he'd load up the plane, fly it to Arizona, fly them to their homes, fly back over to get another load. During the hectic split-second timing of a campaign, this is a man who took time out to sit beside an old friend who was dying of cancer. His campaign managers were understandably impatient, but he said, "There aren't many left who care what happens to her. I'd like her to know I care." This is a man who said to his 19-year-old son, "There is no foundation like the rock of honesty and fairness, and when you begin to build your life on that rock, with the cement of the faith in God that you have, then you have a real start." This is not a man who could carelessly send other people's sons to war. And that is the issue of this campaign that makes all the other problems I've discussed academic, unless we realize we are in a war that must be won.

Those who would trade our freedom for the soup kitchen of the welfare state have told us they have a utopian solution of peace without victory. They call their policy "accommodation." And they say if we only avoid any direct confrontation with the enemy, he will forget his evil ways and learn to love us. All who oppose them are indicted as warmongers. They say we offer simple answers to complex problems. Well, perhaps there is a simple answer—not an easy answer—but simple.

If you and I have the courage to tell our elected officials that we want our national policy based on what we know in our hearts is morally right. We cannot buy our security, our freedom from the threat of the bomb by committing an immorality so great as saying to a billion human beings now enslaved behind the Iron Curtain, "Give up your dreams of freedom because to save our own skins, we are willing to make a deal with your slave masters." Alexander Hamilton said, "A nation which can prefer disgrace to danger is prepared for a master, and deserves one." Now let's set the record straight. There's no argument over the choice between peace and war, but there's only one guaranteed way you can have peace—and you can have it in the next second—surrender.

Admittedly, there's a risk in any course we follow other than this, but every lesson of history tells us that the greater risk lies in appeasement, and this is the specter our well-meaning liberal friends refuse to face—that their policy of accommodation is appeasement, and it gives no choice between peace and war, only between fight or surrender. If we continue to accommodate, continue to back and retreat, eventually we have to face the final demand—the ultimatum. And what then? When Nikita Khrushchev has told his people he knows what our answer will be? He has told them that we are retreating under the pressure of the Cold War, and someday when the time comes to deliver the final ultimatum, our surrender will be voluntary, because by that time we will have been weakened from within spiritually, morally, and economically. He believes this because from our side he's heard voices pleading for "peace at any price" or "better Red than dead," or as one commentator put it, he'd rather "live on his knees than die on his feet." And therein lies the road to war, because those voices don't speak for the rest of us. You and I know and do not believe that life is so dear and peace so sweet as to be purchased at the price of chains and slavery. If nothing in life is worth dying for, when did this begin—just in the face of this enemy? Or should Moses have told the children of Israel to live in slavery under the pharaohs? Should Christ have refused the cross? Should the patriots at Concord Bridge have thrown down their guns and refused to fire the shot heard 'round the world? The martyrs of history were not fools, and our honored dead who gave their lives to stop the advance of the Nazis didn't die in vain. Where, then, is the road to peace? Well it's a simple answer after all. You and I have the courage to say to our enemies, "There is a price we will not pay." "There is a point beyond which they must not advance." This is the meaning in the phrase of Barry Goldwater's "peace through strength." Winston Churchill said, "The destiny of man is not measured by material computations. When great forces are on the move in the world, we learn we are spirits—not animals." And he said, "There's something going on in time and space, and beyond time and space, which, whether we like it or not, spells duty."

You and I have a rendezvous with destiny. We will preserve for our children this, the last best hope of man on earth, or we will sentence them to take the last step into a thousand years of darkness. We will keep in mind and remember that Barry Goldwater has faith in us. He has faith that you and I have the ability and the dignity and the right to make our own decisions and determine our own destiny. Thank you very much.

Freedom Is A Fragile Thing
January 5, 1967

Elected for the first of his two terms as Governor of California, Ronald Reagan gave this speech at his inauguration.

To a number of us, this is a first and hence a solemn and momentous occasion, and yet, on the broad page of state and national history, what is taking place here is almost commonplace routine. We are participating in the orderly transfer of administrative authority by the direction of the people. And this is the simple magic which makes a commonplace routine a near miracle to many of the world's inhabitants: the continuing fact that the people, by democratic process, can delegate this power, yet retain custody of it.

Perhaps you and I have lived with this miracle too long to be properly appreciative. Freedom is a fragile thing and is never more than one generation away from extinction. It is not ours by inheritance; it must be fought for and defended constantly by each generation, for it comes only once to a people. Those who have known freedom and then lost it have never known it again. Knowing this, it is hard to explain those who even today would question the people's capacity for self-rule. Will they answer this: If no one among us is capable of governing himself, then who among us has the capacity to govern someone else? Using the temporary authority granted by the people, an increasing number lately have sought to control the means of production as if this could be done without eventually controlling those who produce. Always this is explained as necessary to the people's welfare. But, "The deterioration of every government begins with the decay of the principle upon which it was founded." This is true today as it was when it was written [by Montesquieu] in 1748.

Government is the people's business, and every man, woman and child becomes a shareholder with the first penny of tax paid. With all the profound wording of the Constitution, probably the most meaningful words are the first three, "We, the People." Those of us here today who have been elected to constitutional office of legislative position are in that three word phrase. We are of the people, chosen by them to see that no permanent structure of government ever encroaches on freedom or assumes a power beyond that freely granted by the people. We stand between the taxpayer and the taxspender.

It is inconceivable to me that anyone could accept this delegated authority without asking God's help. I pray that we who legislate and administer will be granted wisdom and strength beyond our own limited power; that with divine guidance we can avoid easy expedients as we work to build a state where liberty under law and justice can triumph, where compassion can govern and wherein the people can participate and prosper because of their government and not in spite of it.

The path we will chart is not an easy one. It demands much of those chosen to govern, but also from those who did the choosing. And let there be no mistake about this; We have come to a crossroad—a time of decision—and the path we follow turns away from any idea that government and those who serve it are omnipotent. It is a path impossible to follow unless we have faith in the collective wisdom and genius of the people. Along this path government will lead but not rule, listen but not lecture. It is the path of a Creative Society....

For many years now, you and I been shushed like children and told there are no simple answers to the complex problems which are beyond our comprehension.

Well, the truth is, there are simple answers—there just are not easy ones. The time has come for us to decide whether collectively we can afford everything and anything we think of simply because we think of it. The time has come to run a check to see if all the services government provides were is answer to demands or were just goodies dreamed up for our supposed betterment. The time has come to match outgo to income, instead of always doing it the other way around.

The cost of California's government is too high; it adversely affects our business climate. We have a phenomenal growth with hundreds of thousands of people joining us each year. Of course the overall cost of government must go up to provide necessary services for these newcomers, but growth should mean increased prosperity and thus a lightening of the load each individual must bear. If this isn't true, then you and I should be planning how we can put a fence along the Colorado River and seal our borders.

Well, we aren't going to do that. We are going to squeeze and cut and trim until we reduce the cost of government. It won't be easy, nor will it be pleasant, and it will involve every department of government, starting with the Governor's office. I have already informed the Legislature of the reorganization we hope to effect with their help in the executive branch and I have asked for their cooperation and support....

Disraeli said: "Man is not a creature of circumstances. Circumstances are the creatures of men." You and I will shape our circumstances to fit needs.

Let me reaffirm a promise made during the months of campaigning. I believe in your right to know all the facts concerning the people's business. Independent firms are making an audit of state finances. When it is completed, you will have audit. You will have all the information you need to make the decisions which must be made. This is not just a problem for the administration; it is a problem for all of us to solve together. I know that you can face any prospect and do anything that has to be done as long as you know the truth of what you are up against.

We will put our fiscal house in order. And as we do, we will build those things we need to make our state a better place in which to live and we will enjoy them more, knowing we can afford them and they are paid for.

If, in glancing aloft, some of you were puzzled by the small size of our State Flag ... there is an explanation. That flag was carried into battle in Vietnam by young men of California. Many will not be coming home. One did: Sergeant Robert Howell, grievously wounded. He brought that flag back. I thought we would be proud to have it fly over the Capitol today. It might even serve to put our problems in better perspective. It might remind us of the need to give our sons and daughters a cause to believe in and banners to follow.

If this is a dream, it is a good dream, worthy of our generation and worth passing on to the next.

Let this day mark the beginning.

"We Will Be As A City Upon A Hill"
January 25, 1974

Governor Reagan's speech to the Conservative Political Action Conference.

There are men here tonight who, through their wisdom, their foresight and their courage, have earned the right to be regarded as prophets of our philosophy. Indeed they are prophets of our times. In years past when others were silent or too blind to the facts, they spoke up forcefully and fearlessly for what they believed to be right. A decade has passed since Barry Goldwater walked a lonely path across this land reminding us that even a land as rich as ours can't go on forever borrowing against the future, leaving a legacy of debt for another generation and causing a runaway inflation to erode the savings and reduce the standard of living. Voices have been raised trying to rekindle in our country all of the great ideas and principles which set this nation apart from all the others that preceded it, but louder and more strident voices utter easily sold clichés.

Cartoonists with acid-tipped pens portray some of the reminders of our heritage and our destiny as old-fashioned. They say that we are trying to retreat into a past that actually never existed. Looking to the past in an effort to keep our country from repeating the errors of history is termed by them as "taking the country back to McKinley." Of course, I never found that was so bad—under McKinley we freed Cuba. On the span of history, we are still thought of as a young upstart country celebrating soon only our second century as a nation, and yet we are the oldest continuing republic in the world.

I thought that tonight, rather than talking on the subjects you are discussing, or trying to find something new to say, it might be appropriate to reflect a bit on our heritage. You can call it mysticism if you want to, but I have always believed that there was some divine plan that placed this great continent between two oceans to be sought out by those who were possessed of an abiding love of freedom and a special kind of courage.

This was true of those who pioneered the great wilderness in the beginning of this country, as it is also true of those later immigrants who were willing to leave the land of their birth and come to a land where even the language was unknown to them.... Some years ago a writer, who happened to be an avid student of history, told me a story about that day in the little hall in Philadelphia where honorable men, hard-pressed by a King who was flouting the very law they were willing to obey, debated whether they should take the fateful step of declaring their independence from that king. I was told by this man that the story could be found in the writings of Jefferson. I confess, I never researched or made an effort to verify it. Perhaps it is only legend. But story, or legend, he described the atmosphere, the strain, the debate, and that as men for the first time faced the consequences of such an irretrievable act, the walls resounded with the dread word of treason and its price—the gallows and the headman's axe. As the day wore on the issue hung in the balance, and then, according to the story, a man rose in the small gallery. He was not a young man and was obviously calling on all the energy he could muster. Citing the grievances that had brought them to this moment, he said, "Sign that parchment. They may turn every tree into a gallows, every home into a grave and yet the words of that parchment can never die. For the mechanic in his workshop, they will be words of hope, to the slave in the mines—freedom." And he added, "If my hands were freezing in death, I would sign that parchment with my last ounce of strength. Sign, sign if the next moment the noose is around your neck, sign even if the hall is ringing with the sound of headman's axe, for that parchment will be the textbook of freedom, the bible of the rights of man forever." And then it is said he fell back exhausted. But 56 delegates, swept by his eloquence, signed the Declaration of Independence, a document destined to be as immortal as any work of man can be. And according to the story, when they turned to thank him for his timely oratory, he could not be found nor were there any who knew who he was or how he had come in or gone out through the locked and guarded doors.

Well, as I say, whether story or legend, the signing of the document that day in Independence Hall was miracle enough. Fifty-six men, a little band so unique—we have never seen their like since—pledged their lives, their fortunes and their sacred honor. Sixteen gave their lives, most gave their fortunes and all of them preserved their sacred honor. What manner of men were they? Certainly they were not an unwashed, revolutionary rabble, nor were they adventurers in a heroic mood. Twenty-four were lawyers and jurists, 11 were merchants and tradesmen, nine were farmers. They were men who would achieve security but valued freedom more.

And what price did they pay? John Hart was driven from the side of his desperately ill wife. After more than a year of living almost as an animal in the forest and in caves, he returned to find his wife had died and his children had vanished. He never saw them again, his property was destroyed and he died of a broken heart—but with no regret, only pride in the part he had played that day in Independence Hall. Carter Braxton of Virginia lost all his ships—they were sold to pay his debts. He died in rags. So it was with Ellery, Clymer, Hall, Walton, Gwinnett, Rutledge, Morris, Livingston, and Middleton. Nelson, learning that Cornwallis was using his home for a headquarters, personally begged Washington to fire on him and destroy his home—he died bankrupt. It has never been reported that any of these men ever expressed bitterness or renounced their action as not worth the price. Fifty-six rank-and-file, ordinary citizens had founded a nation that grew from sea to shining sea, five million farms, quiet villages, cities that never sleep—all done without an area re-development plan, urban renewal or a rural legal assistance program.

Now we are a nation of 211 million people with a pedigree that includes blood lines from every corner of the world. We have shed that American-melting-pot blood in every corner of the world, usually in defense of someone's freedom. Those who remained of that remarkable band we call our Founding Fathers tied up some of the loose ends about a dozen years after the Revolution. It had been the first revolution in all man's history that did not just exchange one set of rulers for another. This had been a philosophical revolution. The culmination of men's dreams for 6,000 years were formalized with the Constitution, probably the most unique document ever drawn in the long history of man's relation to man. I know there have been other constitutions, new ones are being drawn today by newly emerging nations. Most of them, even the one of the Soviet Union, contain many of the same guarantees as our own Constitution, and still there is a difference. The difference is so subtle that we often overlook it, but it is so great that it tells the whole story. Those other constitutions say, "Government grants you these rights," and ours says, "You are born with these rights, they are yours by the grace of God, and no government on earth can take them from you."

.... In recent years we have been treated to a rash of noble-sounding phrases. Some of them sound good, but they don't hold up under close analysis. Take for instance the slogan so frequently uttered by the young senator from Massachusetts, "The greatest good for the greatest number." ... Every dictator who ever lived has justified the enslavement of his people on the theory of what was good for the majority.

We are not a warlike people. Nor is our history filled with tales of aggressive adventures and imperialism, which might come as a shock to some of the placard painters in our modern demonstrations. The lesson of Vietnam, I think, should be that never again will young Americans be asked to fight and possibly die for a cause unless that cause is so meaningful that we, as a nation, pledge our full resources to achieve victory as quickly as possible. I realize that such a pronouncement, of course, would possibly be laying one open to the charge of warmongering—but that would also be ridiculous. My generation has paid a higher price and has fought harder for freedom than any generation that had ever lived. We have known four wars in a single lifetime. All were horrible, all could have been avoided if at a particular moment in time we had made it plain that we subscribed to the words of John Stuart Mill when he said that "war is an ugly thing, but not the ugliest of things."

The decayed and degraded state of moral and patriotic feeling which thinks nothing is worth a war is worse. The man who has nothing which he cares about more than his personal safety is a miserable creature and has no chance of being free unless made and kept so by the exertions of better men than himself. The widespread disaffection with things military is only a part of the philosophical division in our land today. I must say to you who have recently, or presently are still receiving an education, I am awed by your powers of resistance. I have some knowledge of the attempts that have been made in many classrooms and lecture halls to persuade you that there is little to admire in America. For the second time in this century, capitalism and the free enterprise are under assault. Privately owned business is blamed for spoiling the environment, exploiting the worker and seducing, if not outright raping, the customer. Those who make the charge have the solution, of course—government regulation and control. We may never get around to explaining how citizens who are so gullible that they can be suckered into buying cereal or soap that they don't need and would not be good for them, can at the same time be astute enough to choose representatives in government to which they would entrust the running of their lives.

.... We are told every day that the assembly-line worker is becoming a dull-witted robot and that mass production results in standardization. Well, there isn't a socialist country in the world that would not give its copy of Karl Marx for our standardization. Standardization means production for the masses and the assembly line means more leisure for the worker—freedom from backbreaking and mind-dulling drudgery that man had known for centuries past. Karl Marx did not abolish child labor or free the women from working in the coal mines in England—the steam engine and modern machinery did that.

Unfortunately, the disciples of the new order have had a hand in determining too much policy in recent decades. Government has grown in size and power and cost through the New Deal, the Fair Deal, the New Frontier and the Great Society. It costs more for government today than a family pays for food, shelter and clothing combined.... One Congressman found the federal government was spending 4 billion dollars on research in its own laboratories but did not know where they were, how many people were working in them, or what they were doing. One of the research projects was "The Demography of Happiness," and for 249,000 dollars we found that "people who make more money are happier than people who make less, young people are happier than old people, and people who are healthier are happier than people who are sick." For 15 cents they could have bought an Almanac and read the old bromide, "It's better to be rich, young and healthy, than poor, old and sick."

The course that you have chosen is far more in tune with the hopes and aspirations of our people than are those who would sacrifice freedom for some fancied security. Standing on the tiny deck of the Arabella in 1630 off the Massachusetts coast, John Winthrop said, "We will be as a city upon a hill. The eyes of all people are upon us, so that if we deal falsely with our God in this work we have undertaken and so cause Him to withdraw His present help from us, we shall be made a story and a byword throughout the world." Well, we have not dealt falsely with our God, even if He is temporarily suspended from the classroom.

When I was born my life expectancy was 10 years less than I have already lived—that's a cause of regret for some people in California, I know. Ninety percent of Americans at that time lived beneath what is considered the poverty line today, three-quarters lived in what is considered substandard housing. Today each of those figures is less than 10 percent. We have increased our life expectancy by wiping out, almost totally, diseases that still ravage mankind in other parts of the world. I doubt if the young people here tonight know the names of some of the diseases that were commonplace when we were growing up. We have more doctors per thousand people than any nation in the world. We have more hospitals than any nation in the world. When I was your age, believe it or not, none of us knew that we even had a racial problem. When I graduated from college and became a radio sport announcer, broadcasting major league baseball, I didn't have a Hank Aaron or a Willie Mays to talk about. The Spaulding Guide said baseball was a game for Caucasian gentlemen. Some of us then began editorializing and campaigning against this. Gradually we campaigned against all those other areas where the constitutional rights of a large segment of our citizenry were being denied. We have not finished the job. We still have a long way to go, but we have made more progress in a few years than we have made in more than a century. One-third of all the students in the world who are pursuing higher education are doing so in the United States. The percentage of our young Negro community that is going to college is greater than the percentage of whites in any other country in the world. One-half of all the economic activity in the entire history of man has taken place in this republic. We have distributed our wealth more widely among our people than any society known to man. Americans work less hours for a higher standard of living than any other people. Ninety-five percent of all our families have an adequate daily intake of nutrients—and a part of the five percent that don't are trying to lose weight! Ninety-nine percent have gas or electric refrigeration, 92 percent have televisions, and an equal number have telephones. There are 120 million cars on our streets and highways—and all of them are on the street at once when you are trying to get home at night. But isn't this just proof of our materialism—the very thing that we are charged with? Well, we also have more churches, more libraries, we support voluntarily more symphony orchestras, and opera companies, non-profit theaters, and publish more books than all the other nations of the world put together.

Somehow America has bred a kindliness into our people unmatched anywhere, as has been pointed out in that best-selling record by a Canadian journalist. We are not a sick society. A sick society could not produce the men that set foot on the moon, or who are now circling the earth above us in the Skylab. A sick society bereft of morality and courage did not produce the men who went through those years of torture and captivity in Vietnam. Where did we find such men? They are typical of this land as the Founding Fathers were typical. We found them in our streets, in the offices, the shops and the working places of our country and on the farms. We cannot escape our destiny, nor should we try to do so. The leadership of the free world was thrust upon us two centuries ago in that little hall of Philadelphia. In the days following World War II, when the economic strength and power of America was all that stood between the world and the return to the dark ages, Pope Pius XII said, "The American people have a great genius for splendid and unselfish actions. Into the hands of America God has placed the destinies of an afflicted mankind." We are indeed, and we are today, the last best hope of man on earth.

The Making Of A President
July 17, 1980

The 1980 Republican National Convention, meeting in Detroit, Michigan, nominated Ronald Reagan to be their Presidential candidate. Reagan accepted their nomination with this speech.

My fellow citizens of this great nation: With a deep awareness of the responsibility conferred by your trust, I accept your nomination for the presidency of the United States. I do so with deep gratitude.... And thank you for your wholehearted response to my recommendation in regard to George Bush as a candidate for vice president.

I'm very proud of our party tonight. This convention has shown to all America a party united, with positive programs for solving the nation's problems; a party ready to build a new consensus with all those across the land who share a community of values embodied in these words: family, work, neighborhood, peace and freedom.

.... More than anything else, I want my candidacy to unify our country; to renew the American spirit and sense of purpose. I want to carry our message to every American, regardless of party affiliation, who is a member of this community of shared values.

Never before in our history have Americans been called upon to face three grave threats to our very existence, any one of which could destroy us. We face a disintegrating economy, a weakened defense and an energy policy based on the sharing of scarcity.

The major issue of this campaign is the direct political, personal and moral responsibility of Democratic Party leadership—in the White House and in Congress—for this unprecedented calamity which has befallen us. They tell us they have done the most that humanly could be done. They say that the United States has had its day in the sun; that our nation has passed its zenith. They expect you to tell your children that the American people no longer have the will to cope with their problems; that the future will be one of sacrifice and few opportunities.

My fellow citizens, I utterly reject that view. The American people, the most generous on earth, who created the highest standard of living, are not going to accept the notion that we can only make a better world for others by moving backwards ourselves. Those who believe we can have no business leading the nation.

I will not stand by and watch this great country destroy itself under mediocre leadership that drifts from one crisis to the next, eroding our national will and purpose. We have come together here because the American people deserve better from those to whom they entrust our nation's highest offices, and we stand united in our resolve to do something about it.

We need rebirth of the American tradition of leadership at every level of government and in private life as well. The United States of America is unique in world history because it has a genius for leaders—many leaders—on many levels. But, back in 1976, Mr. Carter said, "Trust me." And a lot of people did. Now, many of those people are out of work. Many have seen their savings eaten away by inflation. Many others on fixed incomes, especially the elderly, have watched helplessly as the cruel tax of inflation wasted away their purchasing power. And, today, a great many who trusted Mr. Carter wonder if we can survive the Carter policies of national defense.

"Trust me" government asks that we concentrate our hopes and dreams on one man; that we trust him to do what's best for us. My view of government places trust not in one person or one party, but in those values that transcend persons and parties. The trust is where it belongs—in the people. The responsibility to live up to that trust is where it belongs, in their elected leaders. That kind of relationship, between the people and their elected leaders, is a special kind of compact.

Three hundred and sixty years ago, in 1620, a group of families dared to cross a mighty ocean to build a future for themselves in a new world. When they arrived at Plymouth, Massachusetts, they formed what they called a "compact"; an agreement among themselves to build a community and abide by its laws.

The single act—the voluntary binding together of free people to live under the law—set the pattern for what was to come.

A century and a half later, the descendants of those people pledged their lives, their fortunes and their sacred honor to found this nation. Some forfeited their fortunes and their lives; none sacrificed honor.

Four score and seven years later, Abraham Lincoln called upon the people of all America to renew their dedication and their commitment to a government of, for and by the people.

Isn't it once again time to renew our compact of freedom; to pledge to each other all that is best in our lives; all that gives meaning to them—for the sake of this, our beloved and blessed land?

Together, let us make this a new beginning. Let us make a commitment to care for the needy; to teach our children the values and the virtues handed down to us by our families; to have the courage to defend those values and the willingness to sacrifice for them.

Let us pledge to restore, in our time, the American spirit of voluntary service, of cooperation, of private and community initiative; a spirit that flows like a deep and mighty river through the history of our nation.

As your nominee, I pledge to restore to the federal government the capacity to do the people's work without dominating their lives. I pledge to you a government that will not only work well, but wisely; its ability to act tempered by prudence and its willingness to do good balanced by the knowledge that government is never more dangerous than when our desire to have it help us blinds us to its great power to harm us.

.... Now make no mistake. We will not permit the safety of our people or our environment heritage to be jeopardized, but we are going to reaffirm that the economic prosperity of our people is a fundamental part of our environment. Our problems are both acute and chronic, yet all we hear from those in positions of leadership are the same tired proposals for more government tinkering, more meddling and more control—all of which led us to this state in the first place. Can anyone look at the record of this administration and say, "Well done?"

Can anyone compare the state of our economy when the Carter Administration took office with where we are today and say, "Keep up the good work?" Can anyone look at our reduced standing in the world today and say, "Let's have four more years of this?"

I believe the American people are going to answer these questions the first week of November and their answer will be, "No—we've had enough." And, then it will be up to us—beginning next January 20th—to offer an administration and congressional leadership of competence and more than a little courage.

We must have the clarity of vision to see the difference between what is essential and what is merely desirable; and then the courage to bring our government back under control.

It is essential that we maintain both the forward momentum of economic growth and the strength of the safety net beneath those in society who need help....

I will not accept the excuse that the federal government has grown so big and powerful that it is beyond the control of any president, any administration or Congress. We are going to put an end to the notion that the American taxpayer exists to fund the federal government. The federal government exists to serve the American people. On January 20th, we are going to reestablish that truth.

Also on that date we are going to initiate action to get substantial relief for our taxpaying citizens and action to put people back to work. None of this will be based on any new form of monetary tinkering or fiscal sleight-of-hand. We will simply apply to government the common sense we all use in our daily lives.

Work and family are at the center of our lives; the foundation of our dignity as a free people. When we deprive people of what they have earned, or take away their jobs, we destroy their dignity and undermine their families. We cannot support our families unless there are jobs; and we cannot have jobs unless people have both money to invest and the faith to invest it.

There are concepts that stem from an economic system that for more than 200 years has helped us master a continent, create a previously undreamed of prosperity for our people and has fed millions of others around the globe. That system will continue to serve us in the future if our government will stop ignoring the basic values on which it was built and stop betraying the trust and good will of the American workers who keep it going.

The American people are carrying the heaviest peacetime tax burden in our nation's history—and it will grow even heavier, under present law, next January. We are taxing ourselves into economic exhaustion and stagnation, crushing our ability and incentive to save, invest and produce.

This must stop. We must halt this fiscal self-destruction and restore sanity to our economic system.

.... The present administration has been forced by us Republicans to play follow-the-leader with regard to a tax cut. But, in this election year we must take with the proverbial "grain of salt" any tax cut proposed by those who have given us the greatest tax increase in our nation's history.

When those in leadership give us tax increases and tell us we must also do with less, have they thought about those who have always had less—especially the minorities? This is like telling them that just as they step on the first rung of the ladder of opportunity, the ladder is being pulled out from under them. That may be the Democratic leadership's message to the minorities, but it won't be ours. Our message will be: We have to move ahead, but we're not going to leave anyone behind.

Thanks to the economic policies of the Democratic Party, millions of Americans find themselves out of work. Millions more have never even had a fair chance to learn new skills, hold a decent job, or secure for themselves and their families a share in the prosperity of this nation.

It's time to put America back to work; to make our cities and towns resound with the confident voices of men and women of all races, nationalities and faiths bringing home to their families a decent paycheck they can cash for honest money. For those without skills, we'll find a way to help them get skills. For those without job opportunities, we'll stimulate new opportunities, particularly in the inner cities where they live.

For those who have abandoned hope, we'll restore hope and we'll welcome them into a great national crusade to make America great again.

When we move from domestic affairs and cast our eyes abroad, we see an equally sorry chapter on the record of the present Administration:

> A Soviet combat brigade trains in Cuba, just 90 miles from our shores.
>
> A Soviet army of invasion occupies Afghanistan, further threatening our vital interests in the Middle East.
>
> America's defense strength is at its lowest ebb in a generation, while the Soviet Union is vastly outspending us in both strategic and conventional arms.
>
> Our European allies, looking nervously at the growing menace from the East, turn to us for leadership and fail to find it.
>
> And, incredibly more than 50 of our fellow Americans have been held captive for over eight months by a dictatorial foreign power that holds us up to ridicule before the world.

Adversaries large and small test our will and seek to confound our resolve, but we are given weakness when we need strength; vacillation when the times demand firmness.

The Carter Administration lives in the world of make-believe. Every day, drawing up a response to that day's problems, troubles, regardless of what happened yesterday and what will happen tomorrow.

But you and I live in the real world, where disasters are overtaking our nation without any real response from Washington.

…. Well, I'll tell you where I stand. I do not favor a peacetime draft or registration, but I do favor pay and benefit levels that will attract and keep highly motivated men and women in our volunteer forces and an active reserve trained and ready for an instant call in case of an emergency.

You know, there may be a sailor at the helm of the ship of state, but the ship has no rudder. Critical decisions are made at times almost in comic fashion, but who can laugh?

Who was not embarrassed when the administration handed a major propaganda victory in the United Nations to the enemies of Israel, our staunch Middle East ally for three decades, and them claim that the American vote was a "mistake," the result of a "failure of communication" between the president, his secretary of state, and his U.N. ambassador?

Who does not feel a growing sense of unease as our allies, facing repeated instances of an amateurish and confused administration, reluctantly conclude that America is unwilling or unable to fulfill its obligations as the leader of the free world? Who does not feel rising alarm when the question in any discussion of foreign policy is no longer, "Should we do something?", but "Do we have the capacity to do anything?"

The Administration which has brought us to this state is seeking your endorsement for four more years of weakness, indecision, mediocrity and incompetence. No. No. No American should vote until he or she has asked, is the United States stronger and more respected now than it was three-and-a-half years ago? Is the world today a safer place in which to live?

It is the responsibility of the President of the United States, in working for peace, to insure that the safety of our people cannot successfully be threatened by a hostile foreign power. As President, fulfilling that responsibility will be my number one priority. We're not a warlike people. Quite the opposite. We always seek to live in peace. We resort to force infrequently and with great reluctance—and only after we have determined that it is absolutely necessary. We are awed—and rightly so—by the forces of destruction at loose in the world in this nuclear era.

But neither can we be naive or foolish. Four times in my lifetime America has gone to war, bleeding the lives of its young men into the sands of beachheads, the fields of Europe and the jungles and rice paddies of Asia. We know only too well that war comes not when the forces of freedom are strong, but when they are weak. It is then that tyrants are tempted.

We simply cannot learn these lessons the hard way again without risking our destruction.

Of all the objectives we seek, first and foremost is the establishment of lasting world peace. We must always stand ready to negotiate in good faith, ready to pursue any reasonable avenue that holds forth the promise of lessening tensions and furthering the prospects of peace. But let our friends and those who may wish us ill take note: the United States has an obligation to its citizens and to the people of the world never to let those who would destroy freedom dictate the future course of human life on this planet. I would regard my election as proof that we have renewed our resolve to preserve world peace and freedom. This nation will once again be strong enough to do that.

Now this evening marks the last step, save one, of a campaign that has taken Nancy and me from one end of this great land to the other, over many months and thousands of miles. There are those who question the way we choose a president; who say that our process imposes difficult and exhausting burdens on those who seek the office. I have not found it so.

It is impossible to capture in words the splendor of this vast continent which God has granted as our portion of this creation. There are no words to express the extraordinary strength and character of this breed of people we call Americans. Everywhere we have met thousands of Democrats, Independents, and Republicans from all economic conditions and walks of life bound together in that community of shared values of family, work, neighborhood, peace and freedom. They are concerned, yes, but they are not frightened. They are disturbed, but not dismayed. They are the kind of men and women Tom Paine had in mind when he wrote, during the darkest days of the American Revolution, "We have it in our power to begin the world over again."

Nearly 150 years after Tom Paine wrote those words, an American president told the generation of the Great Depression that it had a "rendezvous with destiny." I believe that this generation of Americans today has a rendezvous with destiny. Tonight, let us dedicate ourselves to renewing the American compact. I ask you not simply to "Trust me," but to trust your values—our values—and to hold me responsible for living up to them. I ask you to trust that American spirit which knows no ethnic, religious, social, political, regional, or economic boundaries; the spirit that burned with zeal in the hearts of millions of immigrants from every corner of the Earth who came here in search of freedom.

Some say that spirit no longer exists. But I've seen it—I've felt it—all across the land; in the big cities, the small towns and in rural America. It's still there, ready to blaze into life if you and I are willing to do what has to be done; we have to do the practical things, the down-to-earth things, such as creating policies that will stimulate our economy, increase productivity and put America back to work. The time is now to limit Federal spending; to insist on a stable monetary reform and to free ourselves from imported oil.

The time is now to resolve that the basis of a firm and principled foreign policy is one that takes the world as it is and seeks to change it by leadership and example; not by harangue, harassment or wishful thinking.

The time is now to say that while we shall seek new friendships and expand and improve others, we shall not do so by breaking our word or casting aside old friends and allies.

And, the time is now to redeem promises once made to the American people by another candidate, in another time and another place. He said:

> "For three long years I have been going up and down this country preaching that government—Federal, state, and local—costs too much. I shall not stop that preaching. As an immediate program of action, we must abolish useless offices. We must eliminate unnecessary functions of government.
>
> "We must consolidate subdivisions of government and, like the private citizen, give up luxuries which we can no longer afford."

And then he said:

> "I propose to you, my friends, and through you that government of all kinds, big and little be made solvent and that the example be set by the president of the United States and his Cabinet."

That was Franklin Delano Roosevelt's words as he accepted the Democratic nomination for President in 1932.

The time is now, my fellow Americans, to recapture our destiny, to take it into our own hands. But, to do this will take many of us, working together. I ask you tonight to volunteer your help in this cause so we can carry our message throughout the land.

Isn't it time that we, the people, carried out these unkempt promises? Let us pledge to each other and to all America on this July day 48 years later, we intend to do just that.

I have thought of something that is not part of my speech and I'm worried over whether I should do it. Can we doubt that only a Divine Providence placed this land, this island of freedom, here as a refuge for all those people in the world who yearn to breathe free? Jews and Christians enduring persecution behind the Iron Curtain; the boat people of Southeast Asia, of Cuba and Haiti; the victims of drought and famine in Africa, the freedom fighters of Afghanistan and our own countrymen held in savage captivity.

I'll confess that I've been a little afraid to suggest what I'm going to suggest. I'm more afraid not to. Can we begin our crusade joined together in a moment of silent prayer?

God bless America. Thank you.

First Inaugural Address
January 20, 1981

I, Ronald Reagan, do solemnly swear that I will faithfully execute the office of President of the United States, and will, to the best of my ability, preserve, protect, and defend the Constitution of the United States. So help me God.

My fellow citizens: To a few of us here today this is a solemn and most momentous occasion, and yet in the history of our nation it is a commonplace occurrence. The orderly transfer of authority as called for in the Constitution routinely takes place, as it has for almost two centuries, and few of us stop to think how unique we really are. In the eyes of many in the world, this every-four-year ceremony we accept as normal is nothing less than a miracle.

Mr. President [Jimmy Carter], I want our fellow citizens to know how much you did to carry on this tradition. By your gracious cooperation in the transition process, you have shown a watching world that we are a united people pledged to maintaining a political system which guarantees individual liberty to a greater degree than any other, and I thank you and your people for all your help in maintaining the continuity which is the bulwark of our Republic.

The business of our nation goes forward. These United States are confronted with an economic affliction of great proportions. We suffer from the longest and one of the worst sustained inflations in our national history. It distorts our economic decisions, penalizes thrift, and crushes the struggling young and the fixed-income elderly alike. It threatens to shatter the lives of millions of our people.

Idle industries have cast workers into unemployment, human misery, and personal indignity. Those who do work are denied a fair return for their labor by a tax system which penalizes successful achievement and keeps us from maintaining full productivity.

But great as our tax burden is, it has not kept pace with public spending. For decades we have piled deficit upon deficit, mortgaging our future and our children's future for the temporary convenience of the present. To continue this long trend is to guarantee tremendous social, cultural, political, and economic upheavals.

You and I, as individuals, can, by borrowing, live beyond our means, but for only a limited period of time. Why, then, should we think that collectively, as a nation, we're not bound by that same limitation?

We must act today in order to preserve tomorrow. And let there be no misunderstanding—we are going to begin to act, beginning today.

The economic ills we suffer have come upon us over several decades. They will not go away in days, weeks, or months, but they will go away. They will go away because we as Americans have the capacity now, as we've had in the past, to do whatever needs to be done to preserve this last and greatest bastion of freedom.

In this present crisis, government is not the solution to our problem; government is the problem.

From time to time we've been tempted to believe that society has become too complex to be managed by self-rule, that government by an elite group is superior to government for, by, and of the people. Well, if no one among us is capable of governing himself, then who among us has the capacity to govern someone else? All of us together, in and out of government, must bear the burden. The solutions we seek must be equitable, with no one group singled out to pay a higher price.

We hear much of special interest groups. Well, our concern must be for a special interest group that has been too long neglected. It knows no sectional boundaries or ethnic and racial divisions, and it crosses political party lines. It is made up of men and women who raise our food, patrol our streets, man our mines and factories, teach our children, keep our homes, and heal us when we're sick—professionals, industrialists, shopkeepers, clerks, cabbies, and truck drivers. They are, in short, ``We the people," this breed called Americans.

Well, this administration's objective will be a healthy, vigorous, growing economy that provides equal opportunities for all Americans with no barriers born of bigotry or discrimination. Putting America back to work means putting all Americans back to work. Ending inflation means freeing all Americans from the terror of runaway living costs. All must share in the productive work of this ``new beginning," and all must share in the bounty of a revived economy. With the idealism and fair play which are the core of our system and our strength, we can have a strong and prosperous America, at peace with itself and the world.

So, as we begin, let us take inventory. We are a nation that has a government—not the other way around. And this makes us special among the nations of the Earth. Our government has no power except that granted it by the people. It is time to check and reverse the growth of government, which shows signs of having grown beyond the consent of the governed.

It is my intention to curb the size and influence of the Federal establishment and to demand recognition of the distinction between the powers granted to the Federal Government and those reserved to the States or to the people. All of us need to be reminded that the Federal Government did not create the States; the States created the Federal Government.

Now, so there will be no misunderstanding, it's not my intention to do away with government. It is rather to make it work—work with us, not over us; to stand by our side, not ride on our back. Government can and must provide opportunity, not smother it; foster productivity, not stifle it.

If we look to the answer as to why for so many years we achieved so much, prospered as no other people on Earth, it was because here in this land we unleashed the energy and individual genius of man to a greater extent than has ever been done before. Freedom and the dignity of the individual have been more available and assured here than in any other place on Earth. The price for this freedom at times has been high, but we have never been unwilling to pay that price.

It is no coincidence that our present troubles parallel and are proportionate to the intervention and intrusion in our lives that result from unnecessary and excessive growth of government. It is time for us to realize that we're too great a nation to limit ourselves to small dreams. We're not, as some would have us believe, doomed to an inevitable decline. I do not believe in a fate that will fall on us no matter what we do. I do believe in a fate that will fall on us if we do nothing. So, with all the creative energy at our command, let us begin an era of national renewal. Let us renew our determination, our courage, and our strength. And let us renew our faith and our hope.

We have every right to dream heroic dreams. Those who say that we're in a time when there are not heroes, they just don't know where to look. You can see heroes every day going in and out of factory gates. Others, a handful in number, produce enough food to feed all of us and then the world beyond. You meet heroes across a counter, and they're on both sides of that counter. There are entrepreneurs with faith in themselves and faith in an idea who create new jobs, new wealth and opportunity. They're individuals and families whose taxes support the government and whose voluntary gifts support church, charity, culture, art, and education. Their patriotism is quiet, but deep. Their values sustain our national life.

Now, I have used the words ``they" and ``their" in speaking of these heroes. I could say ``you" and ``your," because I'm addressing the heroes of whom I speak—you, the citizens of this blessed land. Your dreams, your hopes, your goals are going to be the dreams, the hopes, and the goals of this administration, so help me God.

We shall reflect the compassion that is so much a part of your makeup. How can we love our country and not love our countrymen; and loving them, reach out a hand when they fall, heal them when they're sick, and provide opportunity to make them self-sufficient so they will be equal in fact and not just in theory?

Can we solve the problems confronting us? Well, the answer is an unequivocal and emphatic ``yes." To paraphrase Winston Churchill, I did not take the oath I've just taken with the intention of presiding over the dissolution of the world's strongest economy.

In the days ahead I will propose removing the roadblocks that have slowed our economy and reduced productivity. Steps will be taken aimed at restoring the balance between the various levels of government. Progress may be slow—measured in inches and feet, not miles—but we will progress. It is time to reawaken this industrial giant, to get government back within its means, and to lighten our punitive tax burden. And these will be our first priorities, and on these principles there will be no compromise.

On the eve of our struggle for independence a man who might have been one of the greatest among the Founding Fathers, Dr. Joseph Warren, president of the Massachusetts Congress, said to his fellow Americans, "Our country is in danger, but not to be despaired of .... On you depend the fortunes of America. You are to decide the important questions upon which rests the happiness and the liberty of millions yet unborn. Act worthy of yourselves."

Well, I believe we, the Americans of today, are ready to act worthy of ourselves, ready to do what must be done to ensure happiness and liberty for ourselves, our children, and our children's children.

And as we renew ourselves here in our own land, we will be seen as having greater strength throughout the world. We will again be the exemplar of freedom and a beacon of hope for those who do not now have freedom.

To those neighbors and allies who share our freedom, we will strengthen our historic ties and assure them of our support and firm commitment. We will match loyalty with loyalty. We will strive for mutually beneficial relations. We will not use our friendship to impose on their sovereignty, for our own sovereignty is not for sale.

As for the enemies of freedom, those who are potential adversaries, they will be reminded that peace is the highest aspiration of the American people. We will negotiate for it, sacrifice for it; we will not surrender for it—now or ever.

Our forbearance should never be misunderstood. Our reluctance for conflict should not be misjudged as a failure of will. When action is required to preserve our national security, we will act. We will maintain sufficient strength to prevail if need be, knowing that if we do so we have the best chance of never having to use that strength.

Above all, we must realize that no arsenal or no weapon in the arsenals of the world is so formidable as the will and moral courage of free men and women. It is a weapon our adversaries in today's world do not have. It is a weapon that we as Americans do have. Let that be understood by those who practice terrorism and prey upon their neighbors.

I'm told that tens of thousands of prayer meetings are being held on this day, and for that I'm deeply grateful. We are a nation under God, and I believe God intended for us to be free. It would be fitting and good, I think, if on each Inaugural Day in future years it should be declared a day of prayer.

This is the first time in our history that this ceremony has been held, as you've been told, on this West Front of the Capitol. Standing here, one faces a magnificent vista, opening up on this city's special beauty and history. At the end of this open mall are those shrines to the giants on whose shoulders we stand.

Directly in front of me, the monument to a monumental man, George Washington, father of our country. A man of humility who came to greatness reluctantly. He led America out of revolutionary victory into infant nationhood. Off to one side, the stately memorial to Thomas Jefferson. The Declaration of Independence flames with his eloquence. And then, beyond the Reflecting Pool, the dignified columns of the Lincoln Memorial. Whoever would understand in his heart the meaning of America will find it in the life of Abraham Lincoln.

Beyond those monuments to heroism is the Potomac River, and on the far shore the sloping hills of Arlington National Cemetery, with its row upon row of simple white markers bearing crosses or Stars of David. They add up to only a tiny fraction of the price that has been paid for our freedom.

Each one of those markers is a monument to the kind of hero I spoke of earlier. Their lives ended in places called Belleau Wood, The Argonne, Omaha Beach, Salerno, and halfway around the world on Guadalcanal, Tarawa, Pork Chop Hill, the Chosin Reservoir, and in a hundred rice paddies and jungles of a place called Vietnam.

Under one such marker lies a young man—Martin Treptow—who left his job in a small town barbershop in 1917 to go to France with the famed Rainbow Division. There, on the western front, he was killed trying to carry a message between battalions under heavy artillery fire. We're told that on his body was found a diary. On the flyleaf under the heading, ``My Pledge," he had written these words: ``America must win this war. Therefore I will work, I will save, I will sacrifice, I will endure, I will fight cheerfully and do my utmost, as if the issue of the whole struggle depended on me alone."

The crisis we are facing today does not require of us the kind of sacrifice that Martin Treptow and so many thousands of others were called upon to make. It does require, however, our best effort and our willingness to believe in ourselves and to believe in our capacity to perform great deeds, to believe that together with God's help we can and will resolve the problems which now confront us.

And after all, why shouldn't we believe that? We are Americans. God bless you, and thank you.

Welcome Home!
January 27, 1981

On November 4, 1979 fifty-two Americans were seized in Tehran, Iran and held as hostages. They were released on January 20, 1981, after four hundred and forty-four days in captivity. One week later, in a White House ceremony, President Reagan welcomed them home.

I can think of no better way to let you know how Nancy and I feel about your presence here today than to say on behalf of us, of the Vice President and Barbara, the Senators, the Members of Congress, the members of the Cabinet, and all of our fellow citizens, these simple words: Welcome home!

You are home, and believe me, you're welcome. If my remarks were a sermon, my text would be lines from the 126th Psalm:

> "We were like those who dreamed. Now our mouth is filled with laughter and our tongue with shouts of joy. The Lord has done great things for us. We are glad."

You've come home to a people who for 444 days suffered the pain of your imprisonment, prayed for your safety, and most importantly, shared your determination that the spirit of free men and women is not a fit subject for barter.

You've represented under great stress the highest traditions of public service. Your conduct is symbolic of the millions of professional diplomats, military personnel, and others who have rendered service to their country.

We're now aware of the conditions under which you were imprisoned. Though now is not the time to review every abhorrent detail of your cruel confinement, believe me, we know what happened. Truth may be a rare commodity today in Iran; it's alive and well in America.

By no choice of your own, you've entered the ranks of those who throughout our history have undergone the ordeal of imprisonment: the crew of the Pueblo, the prisoners in two World Wars and in Korea and Vietnam. And like those others, you are special to us. You fulfilled your duty as you saw it, and now like the others, thank God you're home, and our hearts are full of gratitude.

I'm told that Sergeant Lopez here put up a sign in his cell, a sign that normally would have been torn down by those guards. But this one was written in Spanish, and his guards didn't know that ``Viva la roja, blanco, y azul" means ``Long live the red, white, and blue." They may not understand what that means in Iran, but we do, Sergeant Lopez, and you've filled our hearts with pride. Muchas gracias.

Two days ago, Nancy and I met with your families here at the White House. We know that you were lonely during that dreadful period of captivity, but you were never alone. Your wives and children, your mothers and dads, your brothers and sisters were so full of prayers and love for you that whether you were conscious of it or not, it must have sustained you during some of the worst times. No power on Earth could prevent them from doing that. Their courage, endurance, and strength were of heroic measure, and they're admired by all of us....

Now, I'll not be so foolish as to say forget what you've been through; you never will. But turn the page and look ahead, and do so knowing that for all who served their country, whether in the Foreign Service, the military, or as private citizens, freedom is indivisible. Your freedom and your individual dignity are much cherished. Those henceforth in the representation of this Nation will be accorded every means of protection that America can offer.

Let terrorists be aware that when the rules of international behavior are violated, our policy will be one of swift and effective retribution. We hear it said that we live in an era of limit to our powers. Well, let it also be understood, there are limits to our patience.

... [W]ith us here today are families of the eight heroic men who gave their lives in the attempt to effect your rescue. ``Greater glory hath no man than that he lay down his life for another." And with us also are ... some of the men who did return from that mission. We ask God's special healing for those who suffered wounds and His comfort to those who lost loved one. To them, to you, and to your families, again, welcome from all America and thank you for making us proud to be Americans.

The Man With The Gun
April 28, 1981

On March 30, 1981 a mentally deranged man, John W. Hinckley, Jr., 23, shot and wounded President Reagan. Upon his return to the White House, Ronald Reagan thanked the American people for their thoughts and prayers.

I'd like to say a few words directly to all of you and to those who are watching and listening tonight, because this is the only way I know to express to all of you on behalf of Nancy and myself our appreciation for you messages and flowers and, most of all, your prayers, not only for me but for those others who fell beside me. The warmth of your words, the expression of friendship and, yes, love, meant more to us than you can ever know. You have given us a memory that we'll treasure forever. And you've provided an answer to those few voices that were raised saying that what happened was evidence that ours is a sick society.

The society we heard from is made up of millions of compassionate Americans and their children, from college age to kindergarten. As a matter of fact, as evidence of that I have a letter with me. The letter came from Peter Sweeney. He's in the second grade in the Riverside School in Rockville Centre, and he said, ``I hope you get well quick or you might have to make a speech in your pajamas." He added a postscript. ``P.S. If you have to make a speech in your pajamas, I warned you."

Well, sick societies don't produce men like the two who recently returned from outer space. Sick societies don't produce young men like Secret Service agent Tim McCarthy, who placed his body between mine and the man with the gun simply because he felt that's what his duty called for him to do. Sick societies don't produce dedicated police officers like Tom Delahanty or able and devoted public servants like Jim Brady. Sick societies don't make people like us so proud to be Americans and so very proud of our fellow citizens.

This Last, Best Hope
January 26, 1982

The President shall from time to time give to the Congress information on the State of the Union.

—The United States Constitution

Today marks my first State of the Union address to you, a constitutional duty as old as our Republic itself.

President Washington began this tradition in 1790 after reminding the Nation that the destiny of self-government and the ``preservation of the sacred fire of liberty" is ``finally staked on the experiment entrusted to the hands of the American people." For our friends in the press, who place a high premium on accuracy, let me say: I did not actually hear George Washington say that, but it is a matter of historic record.

From this podium, Winston Churchill asked the free world to stand together against the onslaught of aggression. Franklin Delano Roosevelt spoke of a day of infamy and summoned a nation to arms. Douglas MacArthur made an unforgettable farewell to a country he loved and served so well. Dwight Eisenhower reminded us that peace was purchased only at the price of strength. And John F. Kennedy spoke of the burden and glory that is freedom....

Our foreign policy is a policy of strength, fairness, and balance. By restoring America's military credibility, by pursuing peace at the negotiating table wherever both sides are willing to sit down in good faith, and by regaining the respect of America's allies and adversaries alike, we have strengthened our country's position as a force for peace and progress in the world.

When action is called for, we're taking it. Our sanctions against the military dictatorship that has attempted to crush human rights in Poland—and against the Soviet regime behind that military dictatorship—clearly demonstrated to the world that America will not conduct ``business as usual" with the forces of oppression. If the events in Poland continue to deteriorate, further measures will follow.

Let me also note that private American groups have taken the lead in making January 30th a day of solidarity with the people of Poland—

so, too, the European Parliament has called for March 21st to be an international day of support for Afghanistan. Well, I urge all peace-loving peoples to join together on those days, to raise their voices, to speak and pray for freedom.

Meanwhile, we're working for reduction of arms and military activities. As I announced in my address to the Nation last November 18, we have proposed to the Soviet Union a far-reaching agenda for mutual reduction of military forces and have already initiated negotiations with them in Geneva on intermediate-range nuclear forces.

In those talks it is essential that we negotiate from a position of strength. There must be a real incentive for the Soviets to take these talks seriously. This requires that we rebuild our defenses.

In the last decade, while we sought the moderation of Soviet power through a process of restraint and accommodation, the Soviets engaged in an unrelenting buildup of their military forces. The protection of our national security has required that we undertake a substantial program to enhance our military forces.

We have not neglected to strengthen our traditional alliances in Europe and Asia, or to develop key relationships with our partners in the Middle East and other countries.

Building a more peaceful world requires a sound strategy and the national resolve to back it up. When radical forces threaten our friends, when economic misfortune creates conditions of instability, when strategically vital parts of the world fall under the shadow of Soviet power, our response can make the difference between peaceful change or disorder and violence. That's why we've laid such stress not only on our own defense but on our vital foreign assistance program. Your recent passage of the Foreign Assistance Act sent a signal to the world that America will not shrink from making the investments necessary for both peace and security. Our foreign policy must be rooted in realism, not naiveté or self-delusion.

A recognition of what the Soviet empire is about is the starting point. Winston Churchill, in negotiating with the Soviets, observed that they respect only strength and resolve in their dealings with other nations.

That is why we have moved to reconstruct our national defenses. We intend to keep the peace—we will also keep our freedom.

We have made pledges of a new frankness in our public statements and worldwide broadcasts. In the face of a climate of falsehood and misinformation, we've promised the world a season of truth—the truth of our great civilized ideas: individual liberty, representative government, the rule of law under God.

We've never needed walls or minefields or barbed wire to keep our people in. Nor do we declare martial law to keep our people from voting for the kind of government they want.

Yes, we have our problems; yes, we're in a time of recession. And it's true, there's no quick fix, as I said, to instantly end the tragic pain of unemployment. But we will end it—the process has already begun, and we'll see its effect as the year goes on.

We speak with pride and admiration of that little band of Americans who overcame insuperable odds to set this nation on course 200 years ago. But our glory didn't end with them—Americans ever since have emulated their deeds.

We don't have to turn to our history books for heroes. They're all around us. One who sits among you here tonight epitomized that heroism at the end of the longest imprisonment ever inflicted on men of our Armed Forces. Who will ever forget that night when we waited for television to bring us the scene of that first plane landing at Clark Field in the Philippines—bringing our POW's home? The plane door opened and Jeremiah Denton came slowly down the ramp. He caught sight of our flag, saluted it, said, ``God bless America," and then thanked us for bringing him home.

Just two weeks ago, in the midst of a terrible tragedy on the Potomac, we saw again the spirit of American heroism at its finest—the heroism of dedicated rescue workers saving crash victims from icy waters. And we saw the heroism of one of our young government employees, Lenny Skutnik, who, when he saw a woman lose her grip on the helicopter line, dived into the water and dragged her to safety.

And then there are countless, quiet, everyday heroes of American life—parents who sacrifice long and hard so their children will know a better life than they've known; church and civic volunteers who help to feed, clothe, nurse, and teach the needy; millions who've made our nation and our nation's destiny so very special—unsung heroes who may not have realized their own dreams themselves but then who reinvest those dreams in their children. Don't let anyone tell you that America's best days are behind her—that the American spirit has been vanquished. We've seen it triumph too often in our lives to stop believing in it now.

One hundred and twenty years ago, the greatest of all our Presidents delivered his second State of the Union message in this Chamber. ``We cannot escape history," Abraham Lincoln warned. ``We of this Congress and this administration will be remembered in spite of ourselves." The ``trial through which we pass will light us down, in honor or dishonor, to the latest generation."

That President and that Congress did not fail the American people. Together they weathered the storm and preserved the Union. Let it be said of us that we, too, did not fail; that we, too, worked together to bring America through difficult times. Let us so conduct ourselves that two centuries from now, another Congress and another President, meeting in this Chamber as we are meeting, will speak of us with pride, saying that we met the test and preserved for them in their day the sacred flame of liberty—this last, best hope of man on Earth.

The Sacred Fire Of Liberty
February 26, 1982

President Reagan's speech to the Conservative Political Action Conference.

.... We live today in a time of climactic struggle for the human spirit, a time that will tell whether the great civilized ideas of individual liberty, representative government, and the rule of law under God will perish or endure.

Whittaker Chambers, who sought idealism in communism and found only disillusionment, wrote very movingly of his moment of awakening. It was at breakfast, and he was looking at the delicate ear of his tiny baby daughter, and he said that, suddenly, looking at that, he knew that couldn't just be an accident of nature. He said, while he didn't realize it at the time, he knows now that in that moment God had touched his forehead with his finger.

And later he wrote:

> "For in this century, within the next decades, will be decided for generations whether all mankind is to become Communist, whether the whole world is to become free, or whether in the struggle civilization as we know it is to be completely destroyed or completely changed. It is our fate to live upon that turning point in history."

We've already come a long way together. Thank you for all that you've done for me, for the common values we cherish. Join me in a new effort, a new crusade.

Nostalgia has its time and place. Coming here tonight has been a sentimental journey for me, as I'm sure it has been for many of you. But nostalgia isn't enough. The challenge is now. It's time we stopped looking backward at how we got here.

We must ask ourselves tonight how we can forge and wield a popular majority from one end of this country to the other, a majority united on basic, positive goals with a platform broad enough and deep enough to endure long into the future, far beyond the lifespan of any single issue or personality.

We must reach out and appeal to the patriotic and fundamental ideals of average Americans who do not consider themselves ``movement" people, but who respond to the same American ideals that we do. I'm not talking about some vague notion of an abstract, amorphous American mainstream. I'm talking about "Main Street" Americans in their millions. They come in all sizes, shapes and colors—blue-collar workers, blacks, Hispanics, shopkeepers, scholars, service people, housewives, and professional men and women. They are the backbone of America, and we can't move America without moving their hearts and minds as well.

Fellow Americans, our duty is before us tonight. Let us go forward, determined to serve selflessly a vision of man with God, government for people, and humanity at peace. For it is now our task to tend and preserve, through the darkest and coldest nights, that ``sacred fire of liberty" that President Washington spoke of two centuries ago, a fire that tonight remains a beacon to all the oppressed of the world, shining forth from this kindly, pleasant, greening land we call America.

God bless you, and thank you.

The Crusade For Freedom
June 8, 1982

President Reagan, in a speech to the British Parliament, outlined what would soon become known as "The Reagan Doctrine," American military support for freedom fighters against their Communist governments.

.... We're approaching the end of a bloody century plagued by a terrible political invention—totalitarianism. Optimism comes less easily today, not because democracy is less vigorous, but because democracy's enemies have refined their instruments of repression. Yet optimism is in order, because day by day democracy is proving itself to be a not-at-all-fragile flower. From Stettin on the Baltic to Varna on the Black Sea, the regimes planted by totalitarianism have had more than 30 years to establish their legitimacy. But none—not one regime—has yet been able to risk free elections. Regimes planted by bayonets do not take root.

The strength of the Solidarity movement in Poland demonstrates the truth told in an underground joke in the Soviet Union. It is that the Soviet Union would remain a one-party nation even if an opposition party were permitted, because everyone would join the opposition party....

Historians looking back at our time will note the consistent restraint and peaceful intentions of the West. They will note that it was the democracies who refused to use the threat of their nuclear monopoly in the forties and early fifties for territorial or imperial gain. Had that nuclear monopoly been in the hands of the Communist world, the map of Europe—indeed, the world—would look very different today. And certainly they will note it was not the democracies that invaded Afghanistan or suppressed Polish Solidarity or used chemical and toxin warfare in Afghanistan and Southeast Asia.

If history teaches anything it teaches self-delusion in the face of unpleasant facts is folly. We see around us today the marks of our terrible dilemma—predictions of doomsday, antinuclear demonstrations, an arms race in which the West must, for its own protection, be an unwilling participant. At the same time we see totalitarian forces in the world who seek subversion and conflict around the globe to further their barbarous assault on the human spirit. What, then, is our course? Must civilization perish in a hail of fiery atoms? Must freedom wither in a quiet, deadening accommodation with totalitarian evil?

Sir Winston Churchill refused to accept the inevitability of war or even that it was imminent. He said,

> "I do not believe that Soviet Russia desires war. What they desire is the fruits of war and the indefinite expansion of their power and doctrines. But what we have to consider here today while time remains is the permanent prevention of war and the establishment of conditions of freedom and democracy as rapidly as possible in all countries."

Well, this is precisely our mission today: to preserve freedom as well as peace. It may not be easy to see; but I believe we live now at a turning point.

In an ironic sense Karl Marx was right. We are witnessing today a great revolutionary crisis, a crisis where the demands of the economic order are conflicting directly with those of the political order. But the crisis is happening not in the free, non-Marxist West, but in the home of Marxist-Leninism, the Soviet Union. It is the Soviet Union that runs against the tide of history by denying human freedom and human dignity to its citizens. It also is in deep economic difficulty. The rate of growth in the national product has been steadily declining since the fifties and is less than half of what it was then.

The dimensions of this failure are astounding: a country which employs one-fifth of its population in agriculture is unable to feed its own people. Were it not for the private sector, the tiny private sector tolerated in Soviet agriculture, the country might be on the brink of famine. These private plots occupy a bare 3 percent of the arable land but account for nearly one-quarter of Soviet farm output and nearly one-third of meat products and vegetables. Overcentralized, with little or no incentives, year after year the Soviet system pours its best resource into the making of instruments of destruction. The constant shrinkage of economic growth combined with the growth of military production is putting a heavy strain on the Soviet people. What we see here is a political structure that no longer corresponds to its economic base, a society where productive forces are hampered by political ones.

The decay of the Soviet experiment should come as no surprise to us. Wherever the comparisons have been made between free and closed societies—West Germany and East Germany, Austria and Czechoslovakia, Malaysia and Vietnam—it is the democratic countries what are prosperous and responsive to the needs of their people. And one of the simple but overwhelming facts of our time is this: Of all the millions of refugees we've seen in the modern world, their flight is always away from, not toward the Communist world. Today on the NATO line, our military forces face east to prevent a possible invasion. On the other side of the line, the Soviet forces also face east to prevent their people from leaving.

The hard evidence of totalitarian rule has caused in mankind an uprising of the intellect and will. Whether it is the growth of the new schools of economics in America or England or the appearance of the so-called new philosophers in France, there is one unifying thread running through the intellectual work of these groups—rejection of the arbitrary power of the state, the refusal to subordinate the rights of the individual to the superstate, the realization that collectivism stifles all the best human impulses.

.... Chairman Brezhnev repeatedly has stressed that the competition of ideas and systems must continue and that this is entirely consistent with relaxation of tensions and peace.

Well, we ask only that these systems begin by living up to their own constitutions, abiding by their own laws, and complying with the international obligations they have undertaken. We ask only for a process, a direction, a basic code of decency, not for an instant transformation.

We cannot ignore the fact that even without our encouragement there has been and will continue to be repeated explosions against repression and dictatorships. The Soviet Union itself is not immune to this reality. Any system is inherently unstable that has no peaceful means to legitimize its leaders. In such cases, the very repressiveness of the state ultimately drives people to resist it, if necessary, by force.

While we must be cautious about forcing the pace of change, we must not hesitate to declare our ultimate objectives and to take concrete actions to move toward them. We must be staunch in our conviction that freedom is not the sole prerogative of a lucky few, but the inalienable and universal right of all human beings. So states the United Nations Universal Declaration of Human Rights, which, among other things, guarantees free elections.

The objective I propose is quite simple to state: to foster the infrastructure of democracy, the system of a free press, unions, political parties, universities, which allows a people to choose their own way to develop their own culture, to reconcile their own differences through peaceful means.

This is not cultural imperialism; it is providing the means for genuine self-determination and protection for diversity. Democracy already flourishes in countries with very different cultures and historical experiences. It would be cultural condescension, or worse, to say that any people prefer dictatorship to democracy. Who would voluntarily choose not to have the right to vote, decide to purchase government propaganda handouts instead of independent newspapers, prefer government to worker-controlled unions, opt for land to be owned by the state instead of those who till it, want government repression of religious liberty, a single political party instead of a free choice, a rigid cultural orthodoxy instead of democratic tolerance and diversity?

Since 1917 the Soviet Union has given covert political training and assistance to Marxist-Leninists in many countries. Of course, it also has promoted the use of violence and subversion by these same forces. Over the past several decades, West European and other Social Democrats, Christian Democrats, and leaders have offered open assistance to fraternal, political, and social institutions to bring about peaceful and democratic progress. Appropriately, for a vigorous new democracy, the Federal Republic of Germany's political foundations have become a major force in this effort.

We in America now intend to take additional steps, as many of our allies have already done, toward realizing this same goal. The chairmen and other leaders of the national Republican and Democratic Party organizations are initiating a study with the bipartisan American political foundation to determine how the United States can best contribute as a nation to the global campaign for democracy now gathering force. They will have the cooperation of congressional leaders of both parties, along with representatives of business, labor, and other major institutions in our society. I look forward to receiving their recommendations and to working with these institutions and the Congress in the common task of strengthening democracy throughout the world. It is time that we committed ourselves as a nation—in both the public and private sectors—to assisting democratic development.

…. What I am describing now is a plan and a hope for the long term—the march of freedom and democracy which will leave Marxism-Leninism on the ash-heap of history as it has left other tyrannies which stifle the freedom and muzzle the self-expression of the people. And that's why we must continue our efforts to strengthen NATO even as we move forward with our Zero-Option initiative in the negotiations on intermediate-range forces and our proposal for a one-third reduction in strategic ballistic missile warheads.

Our military strength is a prerequisite to peace, but let it be clear we maintain this strength in the hope it will never be used, for the ultimate determinant in the struggle that's now going on in the world will not be bombs and rockets, but a test of wills and ideas, a trial of spiritual resolve, the values we hold, the beliefs we cherish, the ideals to which we are dedicated.

The British people know that, given strong leadership, time and a little bit of hope, the forces of good ultimately rally and triumph over evil. Here among you is the cradle of self-government, the Mother of Parliaments. Here is the enduring greatness of the British contribution to mankind, the great civilized ideas: individual liberty, representative government, and the rule of law under God.

I've often wondered about the shyness of some of us in the West about standing for these ideals that have done so much to ease the plight of man and the hardships of our imperfect world. This reluctance to use those vast resources at our command reminds me of the elderly lady whose home was bombed in the Blitz. As the rescuers moved about, they found a bottle of brandy she'd stored behind the staircase, which was all that was left standing. And since she was barely conscious, one of the workers pulled the cork to give her a taste of it. She came around immediately and said, "Here now—there now, put it back. That's for emergencies."

Well, the emergency is upon us. Let us be shy no longer. Let us go to our strength. Let us offer hope. Let us tell the world that a new age is not only possible but probable.

During the dark days of the Second World War, when this island was incandescent with courage, Winston Churchill exclaimed about Britain's adversaries, "What kind of a people do they think we are?" Well, Britain's adversaries found out what extraordinary people the British are. But all the democracies paid a terrible price for allowing the dictators to underestimate us. We dare not make that mistake again. So, let us ask ourselves, "What kind of people do we think we are?" And let us answer, "Free people, worthy of freedom and determined not only to remain so but to help others gain their freedom as well."

Sir Winston led his people to great victory in war and then lost an election just as the fruits of victory were about to be enjoyed. But he left office honorably, and, as it turned out, temporarily, knowing that the liberty of his people was more important than the fate of any single leader. History recalls his greatness in ways no dictator will ever know. And he left us a message of hope for the future, as timely now as when he first uttered it, as opposition leader in the Commons nearly 27 years ago, when he said, "When we look back on all the perils through which we have passed and at the mighty foes that we have laid low and all the dark and deadly designs that we have frustrated, why should we fear for our future? We have," he said, "come safely through the worst."

Well, the task I've set forth will long outlive our own generation. But together, we too have come through the worst. Let us now begin a major effort to secure the best—a crusade for freedom that will engage the faith and fortitude of the next generation. For the sake of peace and justice, let us move toward a world in which all people are at last free to determine their own destiny.

A Noble Vision
January 25, 1983

The President shall from time to time give to the Congress information on the State of the Union.

—The United States Constitution

This solemn occasion marks the 196th time that a President of the United States has reported on the State of the Union since George Washington first did so in 1790. That's a lot of reports, but there's no shortage of new things to say about the State of the Union. The very key to our success has been our ability, foremost among nations, to preserve our lasting values by making change work for us rather than against us. I would like to talk with you this evening about what we can do together—not as Republicans and Democrats, but as Americans—to make tomorrow's America happy and prosperous at home, strong and respected abroad, and at peace in the world.

As we gather here tonight, the state of our Union is strong, but our economy is troubled. For too many of our fellow citizens—farmers, steel and auto workers, lumbermen, black teenagers, working mothers—this is a painful period. We must all do everything in our power to bring their ordeal to an end. It has fallen to us, in our time, to undo damage that was a long time in the making, and to begin the hard but necessary task of building a better future for ourselves and our children. We have a long way to go, but thanks to the courage, patience, and strength of our people, America is on the mend....

Nearly half a century ago, in this Chamber, another American President, Franklin Delano Roosevelt, in his second State of the Union message, urged America to look to the future, to meet the challenge of change and the need for leadership that looks forward, not backward.

"Throughout the world," he said, "change is the order of the day. In every nation economic problems long in the making have brought crises to [of] many kinds for which the masters of old practice and theory were unprepared." He also reminded us that "the future lies with those wise political leaders who realize that the great public is interested more in Government than in politics." So, let us, in these next two years—men and women of both parties, every political shade—concentrate on the long-range, bipartisan responsibilities of government, not the short-range or short-term temptations of partisan politics.

.... America's leadership in the world came to us because of our own strength and because of the values which guide us as a society: free elections, a free press, freedom of religious choice, free trade unions, and above all, freedom for the individual and rejection of the arbitrary power of the state. These values are the bedrock of our strength. They unite us in a stewardship of peace and freedom with our allies and friends in NATO, in Asia, in Latin America, and elsewhere. They are also the values which in the recent past some among us had begun to doubt and view with a cynical eye.

Fortunately, we and our allies have rediscovered the strength of our common democratic values, and we're applying them as a cornerstone of a comprehensive strategy for peace with freedom. In London last year, I announced the commitment of the United States to developing the infrastructure of democracy throughout the world. We intend to pursue this democratic initiative vigorously. The future belongs not to governments and ideologies which oppress their peoples, but to democratic systems of self-government which encourage individual initiative and guarantee personal freedom.

But our strategy for peace with freedom must also be based on strength—economic strength and military strength. A strong American economy is essential to the well-being and security of our friends and allies. The restoration of a strong, healthy American economy has been and remains one of the central pillars of our foreign policy. The progress I've been able to report to you tonight will, I know, be as warmly welcomed by the rest of the world as it is by the American people....

A very wise man, Bernard Baruch, once said that America has never forgotten the nobler things that brought her into being and that light her path. Our country is a special place, because we Americans have always been sustained, through good times and bad, by a noble vision—a vision not only of what the world around us is today but what we as a free people can make it be tomorrow.

We're realists; we solve our problems instead of ignoring them, no matter how loud the chorus of despair around us. But we're also idealists, for it was an ideal that brought our ancestors to these shores from every corner of the world.

Right now we need both realism and idealism. Millions of our neighbors are without work. It is up to us to see they aren't without hope. This is a task for all of us. And may I say, Americans have rallied to this cause, proving once again that we are the most generous people on Earth....

Back over the years, citizens like ourselves have gathered within these walls when our nation was threatened; sometimes when its very existence was at stake. Always with courage and common sense, they met the crises of their time and lived to see a stronger, better, and more prosperous country. The present situation is no worse and, in fact, is not as bad as some of those they faced. Time and again, they proved that there is nothing we Americans cannot achieve as free men and women.

Yes, we still have problems—plenty of them. But it's just plain wrong—unjust to our country and unjust to our people—to let those problems stand in the way of the most important truth of all: America is on the mend.

We owe it to the unfortunate to be aware of their plight and to help them in every way we can. No one can quarrel with that. We must and do have compassion for all the victims of this economic crisis. But the big story about America today is the way that millions of confident, caring people—those extraordinary "ordinary" Americans who never make the headlines and will never be interviewed—are laying the foundation, not just for recovery from our present problems but for a better tomorrow for all our people.

From coast to coast, on the job and in classrooms and laboratories, at new construction sites and in churches and community groups, neighbors are helping neighbors. And they've already begun the building, the research, the work, and the giving that will make our country great again.

I believe this, because I believe in them—in the strength of their hearts and minds, in the commitment that each one of them brings to their daily lives, be they high or humble. The challenge for us in government is to be worthy of them—to make government a help, not a hindrance to our people in the challenging but promising days ahead.

If we do that, if we care what our children and our children's children will say of us, if we want them one day to be thankful for what we did here in these temples of freedom, we will work together to make America better for our having been here—not just in this year or this decade but in the next century and beyond.

Thank you, and God bless you.

The Hope And Dream Of Freedom
February 18, 1983

President Reagan's speech to the Conservative Political Action Conference.

…. I believe a feeling of optimism is now entering the American consciousness, a belief that the days of division and discord are behind us and that an era of unity and national renewal is upon us. A vivid reminder of how our nation has learned and grown and transcended the tragedies of the past was given to us here in Washington only a few months ago. Last November, on the Mall, between the Lincoln Memorial and the Washington Monument, a new memorial was dedicated—one of dark, low-lying walls inscribed with the names of those who gave their lives in the Vietnam conflict. Soon, there will be added a sculpture of three infantrymen representing different racial and ethnic backgrounds.

During the dedication ceremonies, the rolls of the missing and dead were read for three days, morning till night, in a candlelight ceremony at the National Cathedral. And those veterans of Vietnam who were never welcomed home with speeches and bands, but who were undefeated in battle and were heroes as surely as any who ever fought in a noble cause, staged their own parade on Constitution Avenue. As America watched them, some in wheelchairs, all of them proud, there was a feeling that as a nation we were coming together, coming together again, and that we had at long last brought the boys home. "A lot of healing … went on," said Jan Scruggs, the wounded combat veteran who helped organize support for the memorial. And then there was this newspaper account that appeared after the ceremonies. I'd like to read it to you.

"Yesterday, crowds returned to the memorial. Among them was Herbie Petit, a machinist and former marine from New Orleans. `Last night,' he said, standing near the wall, `I went out to dinner with some ex-Marines. There was also a group of college students in the restaurant. We started talking to each other, and before we left, they stood up and cheered. The whole week,' Petit said, his eyes red, `it was worth it just for that.'"

It has been worth it. We Americans have learned again to listen to each other, to trust each other. We've learned that government owes the people an explanation and needs their support for its actions at home and abroad. And we've learned—and I pray this time for good—that we must never again send our young men to fight and die in conflicts that our leaders are not prepared to win.

Yet, the most valuable lesson of all, the preciousness of human freedom, has been relearned not just by Americans but all the people of the world. It is "the stark lesson" that Truong Nhu Tang, one of the founders of the National Liberation Front, a former Viet Cong minister and vice-minister of the postwar Vietnamese Communist government, spoke of recently when he explained why he fled Vietnam for freedom. "No previous regime in my country," he wrote about the concentration camps and boat people of Vietnam, "brought such numbers of people to such desperation. Not the military dictators, not the colonialists, not even the ancient Chinese warlords. It is a lesson that my compatriots and I learned through witnessing and through suffering in our own lives the fate of our countrymen. It is a lesson that must eventually move the conscience of the world." This man who had fought on the other side learned the value of freedom only after helping to destroy it and seeing those who had had to give it up. The task that has fallen to us as Americans is to move the conscience of the world, to keep alive the hope and dream of freedom. For if we fail or falter, there'll be no place for the world's oppressed to flee to. This is not a role we sought. We preach no manifest destiny. But like the Americans who brought a new nation into the world 200 years ago, history has asked much of us in our time. Much we've already given; much more we must be prepared to give. This is not a task we shrink from; it's a task we welcome. For with the privilege of living in this kindly, pleasant, greening land called America, this land of generous spirit and great ideals, there is also a destiny and a duty, a duty to preserve and hold in sacred trust mankind's age-old aspirations of peace and freedom and a better life for generations to come. God bless you all, and thank you for what you're doing.

The Evil Empire
March 8, 1983

President Reagan, speaking to the National Association of Evangelicals, made this landmark Cold War speech, labeling the Soviet Union as "The Evil Empire."

.... As good Marxist-Leninists, the Soviet leaders have openly and publicly declared that the only morality they recognize is that which will further their cause, which is world revolution. I think I should point out I was only quoting Lenin, their guiding spirit, who said in 1920 that they repudiate all morality that proceeds from supernatural ideas—that's their name for religion—or ideas that are outside class conceptions. Morality is entirely subordinate to the interests of class war. And everything is moral that is necessary for the annihilation of the old, exploiting social order and for uniting the proletariat.

Well, I think the refusal of many influential people to accept this elementary fact of Soviet doctrine illustrates an historical reluctance to see totalitarian powers for what they are. We saw this phenomenon in the 1930's. We see it too often today.

This doesn't mean we should isolate ourselves and refuse to seek an understanding with them. I intend to do everything I can to persuade them of our peaceful intent, to remind them that it was the West that refused to use its nuclear monopoly in the forties and fifties for territorial gain and which now proposes 50-percent cut in strategic ballistic missiles and the elimination of an entire class of land-based, intermediate-range nuclear missiles.

At the same time, however, they must be made to understand we will never compromise our principles and standards. We will never give away our freedom. We will never abandon our belief in God. And we will never stop searching for a genuine peace. But we can assure none of these things America stands for through the so-called nuclear freeze solutions proposed by some. The truth is that a freeze now would be a very dangerous fraud, for that is merely the illusion of peace. The reality is that we must find peace through strength. I would agree to a freeze if only we could freeze the Soviets' global desires. A freeze at current levels of weapons would remove any incentive for the Soviets to negotiate seriously in Geneva and virtually end our chances to achieve the major arms reductions which we have proposed. Instead, they would achieve their objectives through the freeze.

A freeze would reward the Soviet Union for its enormous and unparalleled military buildup. It would prevent the essential and long overdue modernization of United States and allied defenses and would leave our aging forces increasingly vulnerable. And an honest freeze would require extensive prior negotiations on the systems and numbers to be limited and on the measures to ensure effective verification and compliance. And the kind of a freeze that has been suggested would be virtually impossible to verify. Such a major effort would divert us completely from our current negotiations on achieving substantial reductions.

A number of years ago, I heard a young father, a very prominent young man in the entertainment world, addressing a tremendous gathering in California. It was during the time of the cold war, and communism and our own way of life were very much on people's minds. And he was speaking to that subject. And suddenly, though, I heard him saying, "I love my little girls more than anything." And I said to myself, "Oh, no, don't. You can't—don't say that." But I had underestimated him. He went on: "I would rather see my little girls die now, still believing in God, than have them grow up under communism and one day die no longer believing in God."

There were thousands of young people in that audience. They came to their feet with shouts of joy. They had instantly recognized the profound truth in what he had said, with regard to the physical and the soul and what was truly important.

Yes, let us pray for the salvation of all of those who live in that totalitarian darkness—pray they will discover the joy of knowing God. But until they do, let us be aware that while they preach the supremacy of the state, declare its omnipotence over individual man, and predict its eventual domination of all peoples on the Earth, they are the focus of evil in the modern world.

It was C. S. Lewis who, in his unforgettable Screwtape Letters, wrote: "The greatest evil is not done now in those sordid 'dens of crime' that Dickens loved to paint. It is not even done in concentration camps and labor camps. In those we see its final result. But it is conceived and ordered (moved, seconded, carried and minuted) in clear, carpeted, warmed, and well-lighted offices, by quiet men with white collars and cut fingernails and smooth-shaven cheeks who do not need to raise their voice."

Well, because these "quiet men" do not "raise their voices," because they sometimes speak in soothing tones of brotherhood and peace, because, like other dictators before them, they're always making "their final territorial demand," some would have us accept them at their word and accommodate ourselves to their aggressive impulses. But if history teaches anything, it teaches that simple-minded appeasement or wishful thinking about our adversaries is folly. It means the betrayal of our past, the squandering of our freedom.

So, I urge you to speak out against those who would place the United States in a position of military and moral inferiority. You know, I've always believed that old Screwtape reserved his best efforts for those of you in the church. So, in your discussions of the nuclear freeze proposals, I urge you to beware the temptation of pride—the temptation of blithely declaring yourselves above it all and label both sides equally at fault, to ignore the facts of history and the aggressive impulses of an evil empire, to simply call the arms race a giant misunderstanding and thereby remove yourself from the struggle between right and wrong and good and evil.

I ask you to resist the attempts of those who would have you withhold your support for our efforts, this administration's efforts, to keep America strong and free, while we negotiate real and verifiable reductions in the world's nuclear arsenals and one day, with God's help, their total elimination.

While America's military strength is important, let me add here that I've always maintained that the struggle now going on for the world will never be decided by bombs or rockets, by armies or military might. The real crisis we face today is a spiritual one; at root, it is a test of moral will and faith.

Whittaker Chambers, the man whose own religious conversion made him a witness to one of the terrible traumas of our time, the Hiss-Chambers case, wrote that the crisis of the Western World exists to the degree in which the West is indifferent to God, the degree to which it collaborates in communism's attempt to make man stand alone without God. And then he said, for Marxism-Leninism is actually the second oldest faith, first proclaimed in the Garden of Eden with the words of temptation, "Ye shall be as gods."

The Western World can answer this challenge, he wrote, "but only provided that its faith in God and the freedom He enjoins is as great as communism's faith in Man."

I believe we shall rise to the challenge. I believe that communism is another sad, bizarre chapter in human history whose last pages even now are being written. I believe this because the source of our strength in the quest for human freedom is not material, but spiritual. And because it knows no limitation, it must terrify and ultimately triumph over those who would enslave their fellow man. For in the words of Isaiah:

"He giveth power to the faint; and to them that have no might He increased strength.... But they that wait upon the Lord shall renew their strength; they shall mount up with wings as eagles; they shall run, and not be weary...."

Yes, change your world. One of our Founding Fathers, Thomas Paine, said, "We have it within our power to begin the world over again." We can do it, doing together what no one church could do by itself.

God bless you, and thank you very much.

"Star Wars"
March 23, 1983

President Reagan addressed the nation to announce his plans for an anti-ballistic missile shield, the Strategic Defense Initiative, which soon became known as "Star Wars."

My fellow Americans, thank you for sharing your time with me tonight. The subject I want to discuss with you, peace and national security, is both timely and important. Timely, because I've reached a decision which offers a new hope for our children in the 21st century.... And important because there's a very big decision that you must make for yourselves. This subject involves the most basic duty that any President and any people share, the duty to protect and strengthen the peace....

We and our allies have succeeded in preventing nuclear war for more than three decades. In recent months, however, my advisers, including in particular the Joint Chiefs of Staff, have underscored the necessity to break out of a future that relies solely on offensive retaliation for our security.

Over the course of these discussions, I've become more and more deeply convinced that the human spirit must be capable of rising above dealing with other nations and human beings by threatening their existence. Feeling this way, I believe we must thoroughly examine every opportunity for reducing tensions and for introducing greater stability into the strategic calculus on both sides.

One of the most important contributions we can make is, of course, to lower the level of all arms, and particularly nuclear arms. We're engaged right now in several negotiations with the Soviet Union to bring about a mutual reduction of weapons. I will report to you a week from tomorrow my thoughts on that score. But let me just say, I'm totally committed to this course.

If the Soviet Union will join with us in our effort to achieve major arms reduction, we will have succeeded in stabilizing the nuclear balance. Nevertheless, it will still be necessary to rely on the specter of retaliation, on mutual threat. And that's a sad commentary on the human condition. Wouldn't it be better to save lives than to avenge them? Are we not capable of demonstrating our peaceful intentions by applying all our abilities and our ingenuity to achieving a truly lasting stability? I think we are. Indeed, we must.

After careful consultation with my advisers, including the Joint Chiefs of Staff, I believe there is a way. Let me share with you a vision of the future which offers hope. It is that we embark on a program to counter the awesome Soviet missile threat with measures that are defensive. Let us turn to the very strengths in technology that spawned our great industrial base and that have given us the quality of life we enjoy today.

What if free people could live secure in the knowledge that their security did not rest upon the threat of instant U.S. retaliation to deter a Soviet attack, that we could intercept and destroy strategic ballistic missiles before they reached our own soil or that of our allies?

I know this is a formidable, technical task, one that may not be accomplished before the end of this century. Yet, current technology has attained a level of sophistication where it's reasonable for us to begin this effort. It will take years, probably decades of effort on many fronts. There will be failures and setbacks, just as there will be successes and breakthroughs. And as we proceed, we must remain constant in preserving the nuclear deterrent and maintaining a solid capability for flexible response. But isn't it worth every investment necessary to free the world from the threat of nuclear war? We know it is.

In the meantime, we will continue to pursue real reductions in nuclear arms, negotiating from a position of strength that can be ensured only by modernizing our strategic forces. At the same time, we must take steps to reduce the risk of a conventional military conflict escalating to nuclear war by improving our nonnuclear capabilities.

America does possess—now—the technologies to attain very significant improvements in the effectiveness of our conventional, nonnuclear forces. Proceeding boldly with these new technologies, we can significantly reduce any incentive that the Soviet Union may have to threaten attack against the United States or its allies.

As we pursue our goal of defensive technologies, we recognize that our allies rely upon our strategic offensive power to deter attacks against them. Their vital interests and ours are inextricably linked. Their safety and ours are one. And no change in technology can or will alter that reality. We must and shall continue to honor our commitments.

I clearly recognize that defensive systems have limitations and raise certain problems and ambiguities. If paired with offensive systems, they can be viewed as fostering an aggressive policy, and no one wants that. But with these considerations firmly in mind, I call upon the scientific community in our country, those who gave us nuclear weapons, to turn their great talents now to the cause of mankind and world peace, to give us the means of rendering these nuclear weapons impotent and obsolete.

Tonight, consistent with our obligations of the ABM treaty and recognizing the need for closer consultation with our allies, I'm taking an important first step. I am directing a comprehensive and intensive effort to define a long-term research and development program to begin to achieve our ultimate goal of eliminating the threat posed by strategic nuclear missiles. This could pave the way for arms control measures to eliminate the weapons themselves. We seek neither military superiority nor political advantage. Our only purpose—one all people share—is to search for ways to reduce the danger of nuclear war.

My fellow Americans, tonight we're launching an effort which holds the promise of changing the course of human history. There will be risks, and results take time. But I believe we can do it. As we cross this threshold, I ask for your prayers and your support.

Thank you, good night, and God bless you.

The Beirut Bombing
October 27, 1983

President Reagan spoke to the nation on the deaths of 241 Americans in the October 23, 1983 bombing of the Marine barracks in Beirut, Lebanon.

.... This past Sunday, at 22 minutes after 6 Beirut time, with dawn just breaking, a truck, looking like a lot of other vehicles in the city, approached the airport on a busy, main road. There was nothing in its appearance to suggest it was any different than the trucks or cars that were normally seen on and around the airport. But this one was different. At the wheel was a young man on a suicide mission. The truck carried some 2,000 pounds of explosives, but there was no way our marine guards could know this. Their first warning that something was wrong came when the truck crashed through a series of barriers, including a chain-link fence and barbed wire entanglements. The guards opened fire, but it was too late. The truck smashed through the doors of the headquarters building in which our marines were sleeping and instantly exploded. The four-story concrete building collapsed in a pile of rubble. More than 200 of the sleeping men were killed in that one hideous, insane attack.

.... Brave young men have been taken from us. Many others have been grievously wounded. Are we to tell them their sacrifice was wasted? They gave their lives in defense of our national security every bit as much as any man who ever died fighting in a war. We must not strip every ounce of meaning and purpose from their courageous sacrifice. We're a nation with global responsibilities. We're not somewhere else in the world protecting someone else's interests; we're there protecting our own.... With patience and firmness, we can help bring peace to that strifetorn region—and make our own lives more secure. Our role is to help the Lebanese put their country together, not to do it for them....

May I share something with you I think you'd like to know? It's something that happened to the Commandant of our Marine Corps, General Paul Kelley, while he was visiting our critically injured marines in an Air Force hospital. It says more than any of us could ever hope to say about the gallantry and heroism of these young men, young men who serve so willingly so that others might have a chance at peace and freedom in their own lives and in the life of their country. I'll let General Kelley's words describe the incident. He spoke of:

> "[A] young Marine with more tubes going in and out of his body than I have ever seen in one body. He couldn't see very well. He reached up and grabbed my four stars, just to make sure I was who I said I was. He held my hand with a firm grip. He was making signals, and we realized he wanted to tell me something. We put a pad of paper in his hand—and he wrote 'Semper Fi.' Well, if you've been a Marine or if, like myself, you're an admirer of the marines, you know those words are a battle cry, a greeting, and a legend in the Marine Corps. They're Marine shorthand for the motto of the Corps—'Semper Fidelis'—always faithful."

General Kelley has a reputation for being a very sophisticated general and a very tough marine. But he cried when he saw those words, and who can blame him? That Marine and all those others like him, living and dead, have been faithful to their ideals. They've given willingly of themselves so that a nearly defenseless people in a region of great strategic importance to the free world will have a chance someday to live lives free of murder and mayhem and terrorism. I think that young marine and all of his comrades have given every one of us something to live up to. They were not afraid to stand up for their country or, no matter how difficult and slow the journey might be, to give to others that last, best hope of a better future. We cannot and will not dishonor them now and the sacrifices they've made by failing to remain as faithful to the cause of freedom and the pursuit of peace as they have been.

I will not ask you to pray for the dead, because they're safe in God's loving arms and beyond need of our prayers. I would like to ask you all—wherever you may be in this blessed land—to pray for these wounded young men and to pray for the bereaved families of those who gave their lives for our freedom.

God bless you, and God bless America.

Freedom's Next Step
January 25, 1984

The President shall from time to time give to the Congress information on the State of the Union.

—The United States Constitution

Once again, in keeping with time-honored tradition, I have come to report to you on the state of the Union, and I'm pleased to report that America is much improved, and there's good reason to believe that improvement will continue through the days to come.

You and I have had some honest and open differences in the year past. But they didn't keep us from joining hands in bipartisan cooperation to stop a long decline that had drained this nation's spirit and eroded its health. There is renewed energy and optimism throughout the land. America is back, standing tall, looking to the eighties with courage, confidence, and hope.

The problems we're overcoming are not the heritage of one person, party, or even one generation. It's just the tendency of government to grow, for practices and programs to become the nearest thing to eternal life we'll ever see on this Earth. [Laughter] And there's always that well-intentioned chorus of voices saying, ``With a little more power and a little more money, we could do so much for the people." For a time we forgot the American dream isn't one of making government bigger; it's keeping faith with the mighty spirit of free people under God....

The heart of America is strong; it's good and true. The cynics were wrong; America never was a sick society. We're seeing rededication to bedrock values of faith, family, work, neighborhood, peace, and freedom—values that help bring us together as one people, from the youngest child to the most senior citizen.

The Congress deserves America's thanks for helping us restore pride and credibility to our military. And I hope that you're as proud as I am of the young men and women in uniform who have volunteered to man the ramparts in defense of freedom and whose dedication, valor, and skill increases so much our chance of living in a world at peace.

People everywhere hunger for peace and a better life. The tide of the future is a freedom tide, and our struggle for democracy cannot and will not be denied. This nation champions peace that enshrines liberty, democratic rights, and dignity for every individual. America's new strength, confidence, and purpose are carrying hope and opportunity far from our shores. A world economic recovery is underway. It began here.

We've journeyed far, but we have much farther to go. Franklin Roosevelt told us 50 years ago this month:

> "Civilization cannot go back; civilization must not stand still. We have undertaken new methods. It is our task to perfect, to improve, to alter when necessary, but in all cases to go forward."

It's time to move forward again, time for America to take freedom's next step. Let us unite tonight behind four great goals to keep America free, secure, and at peace in the eighties together.

We can ensure steady economic growth. We can develop America's next frontier. We can strengthen our traditional values. And we can build a meaningful peace to protect our loved ones and this shining star of faith that has guided millions from tyranny to the safe harbor of freedom, progress, and hope....

A lasting and meaningful peace is our ... highest aspiration. And our record is clear: Americans resort to force only when we must. We have never been aggressors. We have always struggled to defend freedom and democracy.

We have no territorial ambitions. We occupy no countries. We build no walls to lock people in. Americans build the future. And our vision of a better life for farmers, merchants, and working people, from the Americas to Asia, begins with a simple premise: The future is best decided by ballots, not bullets.

Governments which rest upon the consent of the governed do not wage war on their neighbors. Only when people are given a personal stake in deciding their own destiny, benefiting from their own risks, do they create societies that are prosperous, progressive, and free. Tonight, it is democracies that offer hope by feeding the hungry, prolonging life, and eliminating drudgery.

When it comes to keeping America strong, free, and at peace, there should be no Republicans or Democrats, just patriotic Americans. We can decide the tough issues not by who is right, but by what is right....

The United States is safer, stronger, and more secure in 1984 than before. We can now move with confidence to seize the opportunities for peace, and we will.

Tonight, I want to speak to the people of the Soviet Union, to tell them it's true that our governments have had serious differences, but our sons and daughters have never fought each other in war. And if we Americans have our way, they never will.

People of the Soviet Union, there is only one sane policy, for your country and mine, to preserve our civilization in this modern age: A nuclear war cannot be won and must never be fought. The only value in our two nations possessing nuclear weapons is to make sure they will never be used. But then would it not be better to do away with them entirely?

People of the Soviet, President Dwight Eisenhower, who fought by your side in World War II, said the essential struggle "is not merely man against man or nation against nation. It is man against war." Americans are people of peace. If your government wants peace, there will be peace. We can come together in faith and friendship to build a safer and far better world for our children and our children's children. And the whole world will rejoice. That is my message to you.

Some days when life seems hard and we reach out for values to sustain us or a friend to help us, we find a person who reminds us what it means to be Americans.

Sergeant Stephen Trujillo, a medic in the 2d Ranger Battalion, 75th Infantry, was in the first helicopter to land at the compound held by Cuban forces in Grenada. He saw three other helicopters crash. Despite the imminent explosion of the burning aircraft, he never hesitated. He ran across 25 yards of open terrain through enemy fire to rescue wounded soldiers. He directed two other medics, administered first aid, and returned again and again to the crash site to carry his wounded friends to safety. Sergeant Trujillo, you and your fellow service men and women not only saved innocent lives;

you set a nation free. You inspire us as a force for freedom, not for despotism; and, yes, for peace, not conquest. God bless you....

How can we not believe in the greatness of America? How can we not do what is right and needed to preserve this last best hope of man on Earth? After all our struggles to restore America, to revive confidence in our country, hope for our future, after all our hard-won victories earned through the patience and courage of every citizen, we cannot, must not, and will not turn back. We will finish our job. How could we do less? We're Americans.

Carl Sandburg said,

> "I see America not in the setting sun of a black night of despair.... I see America in the crimson light of a rising sun fresh from the burning, creative hand of God.... I see great days ahead for men and women of will and vision."

I've never felt more strongly that America's best days and democracy's best days lie ahead. We're a powerful force for good. With faith and courage, we can perform great deeds and take freedom's next step. And we will. We will carry on the tradition of a good and worthy people who have brought light where there was darkness, warmth where there was cold, medicine where there was disease, food where there was hunger, and peace where there was only bloodshed.

Let us be sure that those who come after will say of us in our time, that in our time we did everything that could be done. We finished the race; we kept them free; we kept the faith.

Thank you very much. God bless you, and God bless America.

Peace With Freedom
March 2, 1984

President Reagan's speech to the Conservative Political Action Conference.

…. Peace with freedom is our highest aspiration—a lasting peace anchored by courage, realism, and unity. We've stressed our willingness to meet the Soviets halfway in talks on strategic weapons. But as Commander in Chief, I have an obligation to protect this country, and I will never allow political expediency to influence these crucial negotiations.

We should remember that our defense capability was allowed to deteriorate for many years. Only when our arms are certain beyond doubt can we be certain beyond doubt that they will never be used. President John F. Kennedy spoke those words in 1961. Too many who admired him have forgotten that the price of peace is dear….

And I deeply appreciate your patriotic support for rebuilding our defenses. We're just beginning to restore our capability to meet present and future security needs. I am open to suggestions for budget savings, but defense is not just another Federal program. It is solely the responsibility of the Federal Government. It is its prime responsibility. So, our first responsibility is to keep America strong enough to remain free, secure, and at peace, and I intend to make sure that we do just that.

America's foreign policy supports freedom, democracy, and human dignity for all mankind, and we make no apologies for it. The opportunity society that we want for ourselves we also want for others, not because we're imposing our system on others but because those opportunities belong to all people as God-given birthrights and because by promoting democracy and economic opportunity, we make peace more secure.

Democratic nations do not wage war on their neighbors. But make no mistake, those who would hang a "Do Not Disturb" sign on our shores, those who would weaken America or give Castro's terrorists free rein to bring violence closer and closer to our borders, are doing no service to the cause of peace.

Fellow citizens, fellow conservatives, our time has come again. This is our moment. Let us unite, shoulder to shoulder, behind one mighty banner for freedom. And let us go forward from here not with some faint hope that our cause is not yet lost; let us go forward confident that the American people share our values, and that together we will be victorious.

And in those moments when we grow tired, when our struggle seems hard, remember what Eric Liddell, Scotland's Olympic champion runner, said in *Chariots of Fire,*

> "So where does the power come from to see the race to its end? From within. God made me for a purpose, and I will run for His pleasure."

If we trust in Him, keep His word, and live our lives for His pleasure, He'll give us the power we need—power to fight the good fight, to finish the race, and to keep the faith.

Thank you very much. God bless you, and God bless America.

Vietnam's Unknown Soldier
May 28, 1984

President Reagan gave this speech at Arlington National Cemetery, dedicating the tomb of the Vietnam War's Unknown Soldier.

My fellow Americans, Memorial Day is a day of ceremonies and speeches. Throughout America today, we honor the dead of our wars. We recall their valor and their sacrifices. We remember they gave their lives so that others might live.

We're also gathered here for a special event—the national funeral for an unknown soldier who will today join the heroes of three other wars.

When he spoke at a ceremony at Gettysburg in 1863, President Lincoln reminded us that through their deeds, the dead had spoken more eloquently for themselves than any of the living ever could, and that we living could only honor them by rededicating ourselves to the cause for which they so willingly gave a last full measure of devotion.

Well, this is especially so today, for in our minds and hearts is the memory of Vietnam and all that that conflict meant for those who sacrificed on the field of battle and for their loved ones who suffered here at home. Not long ago, when a memorial was dedicated here in Washington to our Vietnam veterans, the events surrounding that dedication were a stirring reminder of America's resilience, of how our nation could learn and grow and transcend the tragedies of the past.

During the dedication ceremonies, the rolls of those who died and are still missing were read for three days in a candlelight ceremony at the National Cathedral. And the veterans of Vietnam who were never welcomed home with speeches and bands, but who were never defeated in battle and were heroes as surely as any who have ever fought in a noble cause, staged their own parade on Constitution Avenue. As America watched them—some in wheelchairs, all of them proud—there was a feeling that this nation—that as a nation we were coming together again and that we had, at long last, welcomed the boys home.

.... It has been worth it. We Americans have learned to listen to each other and to trust each other again. We've learned that government owes the people an explanation and needs their support for its actions at home and abroad. And we have learned, and I pray this time for good, the most valuable lesson of all—the preciousness of human freedom.

It has been a lesson relearned not just by Americans but by all the people of the world. Yet, while the experience of Vietnam has given us a stark lesson that ultimately must move the conscience of the world, we must remember that we cannot today, as much as some might want to, close this chapter in our history, for the war in Southeast Asia still haunts a small but brave group of Americans—the families of those still missing in the Vietnam conflict.

They live day and night with uncertainty, with an emptiness, with a void that we cannot fathom. Today some sit among you. Their feelings are a mixture of pride and fear. They're proud of their sons or husbands, fathers or brothers who bravely and nobly answered the call of their country. But some of them fear that this ceremony writes a final chapter, leaving those they love forgotten.

Well, today then, one way to honor those who served or may still be serving in Vietnam is to gather here and rededicate ourselves to securing the answers for the families of those missing in action. I ask the Members of Congress, the leaders of veterans groups, and the citizens of an entire nation present or listening, to give these families your help and your support, for they still sacrifice and suffer. Vietnam is not over for them. They cannot rest until they know the fate of those they loved and watched march off to serve their country. Our dedication to their cause must be strengthened with these events today. We write no last chapters. We close no books. We put away no final memories. An end to America's involvement in Vietnam cannot come before we've achieved the fullest possible accounting of those missing in action.

This can only happen when their families know with certainty that this nation discharged her duty to those who served nobly and well. Today a united people call upon Hanoi with one voice: Heal the sorest wound of this conflict. Return our sons to America. End the grief of those who are innocent and undeserving of any retribution.

The Unknown Soldier who is returned to us today and whom we lay to rest is symbolic of all our missing sons, and we will present him with the Congressional Medal of Honor, the highest military decoration that we can bestow. About him we may well wonder, as others have: As a child, did he play on some street in a great American city? Or did he work beside his father on a farm out in America's heartland? Did he marry? Did he have children? Did he look expectantly to return to a bride?

We'll never know the answers to these questions about his life. We do know, though, why he died. He saw the horrors of war but bravely faced them, certain his own cause and his country's cause was a noble one; that he was fighting for human dignity, for free men everywhere. Today we pause to embrace him and all who served us so well in a war whose end offered no parades, no flags, and so little thanks. We can be worthy of the values and ideals for which our sons sacrificed—worthy of their courage in the face of a fear that few of us will ever experience—by honoring their commitment and devotion to duty and country.

Many veterans of Vietnam still serve in the Armed Forces, work in our offices, on our farms, and in our factories. Most have kept their experiences private, but most have been strengthened by their call to duty. A grateful nation opens her heart today in gratitude for their sacrifice, for their courage, and for their noble service. Let us, if we must, debate the lessons learned at some other time. Today, we simply say with pride,

> "Thank you, dear son. May God cradle you in His loving arms."

We present to you our nation's highest award, the Congressional Medal of Honor, for service above and beyond the call of duty in action with the enemy during the Vietnam era. Thank you.

The Fortieth Anniversary Of D-Day
June 6, 1984

President Reagan marked the fortieth anniversary of the D-Day invasion with this speech at Normandy's Pointe du Hoc.

We're here to mark that day in history when the Allied armies joined in battle to reclaim this continent to liberty. For four long years, much of Europe had been under a terrible shadow. Free nations had fallen, Jews cried out in the camps, millions cried out for liberation. Europe was enslaved, and the world prayed for its rescue. Here in Normandy the rescue began. Here the Allies stood and fought against tyranny in a giant undertaking unparalleled in human history.

We stand on a lonely, windswept point on the northern shore of France. The air is soft, but 40 years ago at this moment, the air was dense with smoke and the cries of men, and the air was filled with the crack of rifle fire and the roar of cannon. At dawn, on the morning of the 6th of June, 1944, 225 Rangers jumped off the British landing craft and ran to the bottom of these cliffs. Their mission was one of the most difficult and daring of the invasion: to climb these sheer and desolate cliffs and take out the enemy guns. The Allies had been told that some of the mightiest of these guns were here and they would be trained on the beaches to stop the Allied advance.

The Rangers looked up and saw the enemy soldiers—at the edge of the cliffs shooting down at them with machineguns and throwing grenades. And the American Rangers began to climb. They shot rope ladders over the face of these cliffs and began to pull themselves up. When one Ranger fell, another would take his place. When one rope was cut, a Ranger would grab another and begin his climb again. They climbed, shot back, and held their footing. Soon, one by one, the Rangers pulled themselves over the top, and in seizing the firm land at the top of these cliffs, they began to seize back the continent of Europe. Two hundred and twenty-five came here. After two days of fighting, only ninety could still bear arms.

Behind me is a memorial that symbolizes the Ranger daggers that were thrust into the top of these cliffs. And before me are the men who put them there.

These are the boys of Pointe du Hoc. These are the men who took the cliffs. These are the champions who helped free a continent. These are the heroes who helped end a war. Gentlemen, I look at you and I think of the words of Stephen Spender's poem. You are men who in your "lives fought for life … and left the vivid air signed with your honor."

…. Forty summers have passed since the battle that you fought here. You were young the day you took these cliffs; some of you were hardly more than boys, with the deepest joys of life before you. Yet, you risked everything here. Why? Why did you do it? What impelled you to put aside the instinct for self-preservation and risk your lives to take these cliffs? What inspired all the men of the armies that met here? We look at you, and somehow we know the answer. It was faith and belief; it was loyalty and love.

The men of Normandy had faith that what they were doing was right, faith that they fought for all humanity, faith that a just God would grant them mercy on this beachhead or on the next. It was the deep knowledge—and pray God we have not lost it—that there is a profound, moral difference between the use of force for liberation and the use of force for conquest. You were here to liberate, not to conquer, and so you and those others did not doubt your cause. And you were right not to doubt.

You all knew that some things are worth dying for. One's country is worth dying for, and democracy is worth dying for, because it's the most deeply honorable form of government ever devised by man. All of you loved liberty. All of you were willing to fight tyranny, and you knew the people of your countries were behind you….

Thank you very much, and God bless you all.

President Reagan marked the fortieth anniversary of the D-Day invasion with this second speech at Normandy's Omaha Beach.

Mr. President, distinguished guests, we stand today at a place of battle, one that forty years ago saw and felt the worst of war. Men bled and died here for a few feet of—or inches of—sand, as bullets and shellfire cut through their ranks. About them, General Omar Bradley later said, "Every man who set foot on Omaha Beach that day was a hero."

No speech can adequately portray their suffering, their sacrifice, their heroism. President Lincoln once reminded us that through their deeds, the dead of battle have spoken more eloquently for themselves than any of the living ever could. But we can only honor them by rededicating ourselves to the cause for which they gave a last full measure of devotion.

Today we do rededicate ourselves to that cause. And at this place of honor, we're humbled by the realization of how much so many gave to the cause of freedom and to their fellow man.

Some who survived the battle of June 6, 1944, are here today. Others who hoped to return never did. "Someday, Lis, I'll go back," said Private First Class Peter Robert Zanatta, of the 37th Engineer Combat Battalion, and first assault wave to hit Omaha Beach. "I'll go back, and I'll see it all again. I'll see the beach, the barricades, and the graves."

Those words of Private Zanatta come to us from his daughter, Lisa Zanatta Henn, in a heart-rending story about the event her father spoke of so often. "In his words, the Normandy invasion would change his life forever," she said. She tells some of his stories of World War II but says of her father, "the story to end all stories was D-Day."

"He made me feel the fear of being on that boat waiting to land. I can smell the ocean and feel the seasickness. I can see the looks on his fellow soldiers' faces—the fear, the anguish, the uncertainty of what lay ahead. And when they landed, I can feel the strength and courage of the men who took those first steps through the tide to what must have surely looked like instant death."

Private Zanatta's daughter wrote to me: "I don't know how or why I can feel this emptiness, this fear, or this determination, but I do. Maybe it's the bond I had with my father. All I know is that it brings tears to my eyes to think about my father as a twenty-year-old boy having to face that beach."

The anniversary of D-Day was always special for her family. And like all the families of those who went to war, she describes how she came to realize her own father's survival was a miracle: "So many men died. I know that my father watched many of his friends be killed. I know that he must have died inside a little each time. But his explanation to me was, `You did what you had to do, and you kept on going.'"

When men like Private Zanatta and all our allied forces stormed the beaches of Normandy forty years ago they came not as conquerors, but as liberators. When these troops swept across the French countryside and into the forests of Belgium and Luxembourg they came not to take, but to return what had been wrongly seized. When our forces marched into Germany they came not to prey on a brave and defeated people, but to nurture the seeds of democracy among those who yearned to be free again.

We salute them today. But, Mr. President, we also salute those who, like yourself, were already engaging the enemy inside your beloved country—the French Resistance. Your valiant struggle for France did so much to cripple the enemy and spur the advance of the armies of liberation. The French Forces of the Interior will forever personify courage and national spirit. They will be a timeless inspiration to all who are free and to all who would be free.

Today, in their memory, and for all who fought here, we celebrate the triumph of democracy. We reaffirm the unity of democratic peoples who fought a war and then joined with the vanquished in a firm resolve to keep the peace.

From a terrible war we learned that unity made us invincible; now, in peace, that same unity makes us secure. We sought to bring all freedom-loving nations together in a community dedicated to the defense and preservation of our sacred values. Our alliance, forged in the crucible of war, tempered and shaped by the realities of the postwar world, has succeeded. In Europe, the threat has been contained, the peace has been kept.

Today the living here assembled—officials, veterans, citizens—are a tribute to what was achieved here 40 years ago. This land is secure. We are free. These things are worth fighting and dying for.

Lisa Zanatta Henn began her story by quoting her father, who promised that he would return to Normandy. She ended with a promise to her father, who died eight years ago of cancer: "I'm going there, Dad, and I'll see the beaches and the barricades and the monuments. I'll see the graves, and I'll put flowers there just like you wanted to do. I'll feel all the things you made me feel through your stories and your eyes. I'll never forget what you went through, Dad, nor will I let anyone else forget. And, Dad, I'll always be proud."

Through the words of his loving daughter, who is here with us today, a D-day veteran has shown us the meaning of this day far better than any President can. It is enough for us to say about Private Zanatta and all the men of honor and courage who fought beside him four decades ago: We will always remember. We will always be proud. We will always be prepared, so we may always be free. Thank you.

This Springtime Of Hope
August 23, 1984

President Reagan's acceptance speech at the Republican National Convention.

.... In 1980 we asked the people of America, "Are you better off than you were four years ago?" Well, the people answered then by choosing us to bring about a change. We have every reason now, four years later, to ask that same question again, for we have made a change.

The American people joined us and helped us. Let us ask for their help again to renew the mandate of 1980, to move us further forward on the road we presently travel, the road of common sense, of people in control of their own destiny; the road leading to prosperity and economic expansion in a world at peace.

As we ask for their help, we should also answer the central question of public service: Why are we here? What do we believe in? Well for one thing, we're here to see that government continues to serve the people and not the other way around. Yes, government should do all that is necessary, but only that which is necessary.

We don't lump people by groups or special interests. And let me add, in the party of Lincoln, there is no room for intolerance and not even a small corner for anti-Semitism or bigotry of any kind. Many people are welcome in our house, but not the bigots.

We believe in the uniqueness of each individual. We believe in the sacredness of human life. For some time now we've all fallen into a pattern of describing our choice as left or right. It's become standard rhetoric in discussions of political philosophy. But is that really an accurate description of the choice before us?

Go back a few years to the origin of the terms and see where left or right would take us if we continued far enough in either direction. Stalin. Hitler. One would take us to Communist totalitarianism; the other to the totalitarianism of Hitler.

Isn't our choice really not one of left or right, but of up or down? Down through the welfare state to statism, to more and more government largesse accompanied always by more government authority, less individual liberty and, ultimately, totalitarianism, always advanced as for our own good. The alternative is the dream conceived by our Founding Fathers, up to the ultimate in individual freedom consistent with an orderly society.

We don't celebrate dependence day on the Fourth of July. We celebrate Independence Day.

We celebrate the right of each individual to be recognized as unique, possessed of dignity and the sacred right to life, liberty, and the pursuit of happiness. At the same time, with our independence goes a generosity of spirit more evident here than in almost any other part of the world. Recognizing the equality of all men and women, we're willing and able to lift the weak, cradle those who hurt, and nurture the bonds that tie us together as one nation under God.

Finally, we're here to shield our liberties, not just for now or for a few years but forever.

Could I share a personal thought with you tonight, because tonight's kind of special to me. It's the last time, of course, that I will address you under these same circumstances. I hope you'll invite me back to future conventions. Nancy and I will be forever grateful for the honor you've done us, for the opportunity to serve, and for your friendship and trust.

I began political life as a Democrat, casting my first vote in 1932 for Franklin Delano Roosevelt. That year, the Democrats called for a 25-percent reduction in the cost of government by abolishing useless commissions and offices and consolidating departments and bureaus, and giving more authority to State governments. As the years went by and those promises were forgotten, did I leave the Democratic Party, or did the leadership of that party leave not just me but millions of patriotic Democrats who believed in the principles and philosophy of that platform?

One of the first to declare this was a former Democratic nominee for President—Al Smith, the Happy Warrior, who went before the Nation in 1936 to say ... that he could no longer follow his party's leadership and that he was "taking a walk." As Democratic leaders have taken their party further and further away from its first principles, it's no surprise that so many responsible Democrats feel that our platform is closer to their views, and we welcome them to our side.

Four years ago we raised a banner of bold colors—no pale pastels. We proclaimed a dream of an America that would be "a shining city on a hill."

We promised that we'd reduce the growth of the Federal Government, and we have. We said we intended to reduce interest rates and inflation, and we have. We said we would reduce taxes to provide incentives for individuals and business to get our economy moving again, and we have. We said there must be jobs with a future for our people, not government make-work programs, and, in the last nineteen months, as I've said, 6-1/2 million new jobs in the private sector have been created. We said we would once again be respected throughout the world, and we are. We said we would restore our ability to protect our freedom on land, sea, and in the air, and we have.

We bring to the American citizens in this election year a record of accomplishment and the promise of continuation.

We came together in a national crusade to make America great again, and to make a new beginning. Well, now it's all coming together. With our beloved nation at peace, we're in the midst of a springtime of hope for America. Greatness lies ahead of us.

Holding the Olympic games here in the United States began defining the promise of this season. All through the spring and summer, we marveled at the journey of the Olympic torch as it made its passage east to west. Over 9,000 miles, by some 4,000 runners, that flame crossed a portrait of our nation.

From our Gotham City, New York, to the Cradle of Liberty, Boston, across the Appalachian springtime, to the City of the Big Shoulders, Chicago. Moving south toward Atlanta, over to St. Louis, past its Gateway Arch, across wheatfields into the stark beauty of the Southwest and then up into the still, snowcapped Rockies. And, after circling the greening Northwest, it came down to California, across the Golden Gate and finally into Los Angeles. And all along the way, that torch became a celebration of America. And we all became participants in the celebration.

Each new story was typical of this land of ours. There was Ansel Stubbs, a youngster of 99, who passed the torch in Kansas to four-year-old Katie Johnson. In Pineville, Kentucky, it came at 1 a.m., so hundreds of people lined the streets with candles. At Tupelo, Mississippi, at 7 a.m. on a Sunday morning, a robed church choir sang "God Bless America" as the torch went by. That torch went through the Cumberland Gap, past the Martin Luther King, Jr., Memorial, down the Santa Fe Trail, and alongside Billy the Kid's grave.

In Richardson, Texas, it was carried by a fourteen-year-old boy in a special wheelchair. In West Virginia the runner came across a line of deaf children and let each one pass the torch for a few feet, and at the end these youngsters' hands talked excitedly in their sign language. Crowds spontaneously began singing "America the Beautiful" or "The Battle Hymn of the Republic."

And then, in San Francisco a Vietnamese immigrant, his little son held on his shoulders, dodged photographers and policemen to cheer a nineteen-year-old black man pushing an eighty-eight-year-old white woman in a wheelchair as she carried the torch.

My friends, that's America.

We cheered in Los Angeles as the flame was carried in and the giant Olympic torch burst into a billowing fire in front of the teams, the youth of 140 nations assembled on the floor of the Coliseum. And in that moment, maybe you were struck as I was with the uniqueness of what was taking place before a hundred thousand people in the stadium, most of them citizens of our country, and over a billion worldwide watching on television. There were athletes representing 140 countries here to compete in the one country in all the world whose people carry the bloodlines of all those 140 countries and more. Only in the United States is there such a rich mixture of races, creeds, and nationalities—only in our melting pot.

And that brings to mind another torch, the one that greeted so many of our parents and grandparents. Just this past Fourth of July, the torch atop the Statue of Liberty was hoisted down for replacement. We can be forgiven for thinking that maybe it was just worn out from lighting the way to freedom for seventeen million new Americans. So, now we'll put up a new one.

The poet called Miss Liberty's torch the "lamp beside the golden door." Well, that was the entrance to America, and it still is. And now you really know why we're here tonight. The glistening hope of that lamp is still ours. Every promise, every opportunity is still golden in this land. And through that golden door our children can walk into tomorrow with the knowledge that no one can be denied the promise that is America.

Her heart is full; her door is still golden, her future bright. She has arms big enough to comfort and strong enough to support, for the strength in her arms is the strength of her people. She will carry on in the eighties unafraid, unashamed, and unsurpassed.

In this springtime of hope, some lights seem eternal; America's is.

Thank you, God bless you, and God bless America.

Second Inaugural Address
January 21, 1985

I, Ronald Reagan, do solemnly swear that I will faithfully execute the office of President of the United States, and will, to the best of my ability, preserve, protect, and defend the Constitution of the United States. So help me God.

My fellow citizens: .... This is ... the fiftieth time that we, the people, have celebrated this historic occasion. When the first President, George Washington, placed his hand upon the Bible, he stood less than a single day's journey by horseback from raw, untamed wilderness. There were 4 million Americans in a union of thirteen States. Today, we are sixty times as many in a union of fifty States. We've lighted the world with our inventions, gone to the aid of mankind wherever in the world there was a cry for help, journeyed to the Moon and safely returned. So much has changed, and yet we stand together as we did two centuries ago.

When I took this oath four years ago, I did so in a time of economic stress. Voices were raised saying that we had to look to our past for the greatness and glory. But we, the present-day Americans, are not given to looking backward. In this blessed land, there is always a better tomorrow.

Four years ago, I spoke to you of a New Beginning, and we have accomplished that. But in another sense, our New Beginning is a continuation of that beginning created two centuries ago when, for the first time in history, government, the people said, was not our master, it is our servant; its only power that which we the people allow it to have.

That system has never failed us, but for a time we failed the system. We asked things of government that government was not equipped to give. We yielded authority to the National Government that properly belonged to States or to local governments or to the people themselves. We allowed taxes and inflation to rob us of our earnings and savings and watched the great industrial machine that had made us the most productive people on Earth slow down and the number of unemployed increase. By 1980 we knew it was time to renew our faith, to strive with all our strength toward the ultimate in individual freedom, consistent with an orderly society.

We believed then and now—there are no limits to growth and human progress when men and women are free to follow their dreams. And we were right to believe that. Tax rates have been reduced, inflation cut dramatically, and more people are employed than ever before in our history.

We are creating a nation once again vibrant, robust, and alive. But there are many mountains yet to climb. We will not rest until every American enjoys the fullness of freedom, dignity, and opportunity as our birthright. It is our birthright as citizens of this great Republic.

And if we meet this challenge, these will be years when Americans have restored their confidence and tradition of progress; when our values of faith, family, work, and neighborhood were restated for a modern age; when our economy was finally freed from government's grip; when we made sincere efforts at meaningful arms reductions and by rebuilding our defenses, our economy, and developing new technologies, helped preserve peace in a troubled world; when America courageously supported the struggle for individual liberty, self-government, and free enterprise throughout the world and turned the tide of history away from totalitarian darkness and into the warm sunlight of human freedom.

My fellow citizens, our nation is poised for greatness. We must do what we know is right, and do it with all our might. Let history say of us, "These were golden years—when the American Revolution was reborn, when freedom gained new life, and America reached for her best.

Our two-party system has solved us—served us, I should say, well over the years, but never better than in those times of great challenge when we came together not as Democrats or Republicans, but as Americans united in a common cause.

Two of our Founding Fathers, a Boston lawyer named Adams and a Virginia planter named Jefferson, members of that remarkable group who met in Independence Hall and dared to think they could start the world over again, left us an important lesson. They had become ... political rivals in the Presidential election of 1800. Then, years later, when both were retired and age had softened their anger, they began to speak to each other again through letters. A bond was reestablished between those two who had helped create this government of ours.

In 1826, the fiftieth anniversary of the Declaration of Independence, they both died. They died on the same day, within a few hours of each other, and that day was the Fourth of July.

In one of those letters exchanged in the sunset of their lives, Jefferson wrote:

"It carries me back to the times when, beset with difficulties and dangers, we were fellow laborers in the same cause, struggling for what is most valuable to man, his right of self-government. Laboring always at the same oar, with some wave ever ahead threatening to overwhelm us, and yet passing harmless ... we rode through the storm with heart and hand."

Well, with heart and hand let us stand as one today—one people under God, determined that our future shall be worthy of our past. As we do, we must not repeat the well-intentioned errors of our past. We must never again abuse the trust of working men and women by sending their earnings on a futile chase after the spiraling demands of a bloated Federal Establishment. You elected us in 1980 to end this prescription for disaster, and I don't believe you reelected us in 1984 to reverse course.

At the heart of our efforts is one idea vindicated by twenty-five straight months of economic growth—freedom and incentives unleash the drive and entrepreneurial genius that are the core of human progress. We have begun to increase the rewards for work, savings, and investment; reduce the increase in the cost and size of government and its interference in people's lives.

We must simplify our tax system, make it more fair and bring the rates down for all who work and earn. We must think anew and move with a new boldness, so every American who seeks work can find work, so the least among us shall have an equal chance to achieve the greatest things—to be heroes who heal our sick, feed the hungry, protect peace among nations, and leave this world a better place.

The time has come for a new American emancipation—a great national drive to tear down economic barriers and liberate the spirit of enterprise in the most distressed areas of our country. My friends, together we can do this, and do it we must, so help me God.

From new freedom will spring new opportunities for growth, a more productive, fulfilled, and united people, and a stronger America—an America that will lead the technological revolution and also open its mind and heart and soul to the treasures of literature, music, and poetry, and the values of faith, courage, and love.

A dynamic economy, with more citizens working and paying taxes, will be our strongest tool to bring down budget deficits. But an almost unbroken fifty years of deficit spending has finally brought us to a time of reckoning. We've come to a turning point, a moment for hard decisions. I have asked the Cabinet and my staff a question and now I put the same question to all of you. If not us, who? And if not now, when? It must be done by all of us going forward with a program aimed at reaching a balanced budget. We can then begin reducing the national debt.

I will shortly submit a budget to the Congress aimed at freezing government program spending for the next year. Beyond this, we must take further steps to permanently control government's power to tax and spend. We must act now to protect future generations from government's desire to spend its citizens' money and tax them into servitude when the bills come due. Let us make it unconstitutional for the Federal Government to spend more than the Federal Government takes in.

We have already started returning to the people and to State and local governments responsibilities better handled by them. Now, there is a place for the Federal Government in matters of social compassion. But our fundamental goals must be to reduce dependency and upgrade the dignity of those who are infirm or disadvantaged. And here, a growing economy and support from family and community offer our best chance for a society where compassion is a way of life, where the old and infirm are cared for, the young and, yes, the unborn protected, and the unfortunate looked after and made self-sufficient.

Now, there is another area where the Federal Government can play a part. As an older American, I remember a time when people of different race, creed, or ethnic origin in our land found hatred and prejudice installed in social custom and, yes, in law. There's no story more heartening in our history than the progress that we've made toward the brotherhood of man that God intended for us. Let us resolve there will be no turning back or hesitation on the road to an America rich in dignity and abundant with opportunity for all our citizens.

Let us resolve that we, the people, will build an American opportunity society in which all of us—white and black, rich and poor, young and old—will go forward together, arm in arm. Again, let us remember that though our heritage is one of blood lines from every corner of the Earth, we are all Americans, pledged to carry on this last, best hope of man on Earth.

I've spoken of our domestic goals and the limitations we should put on our National Government. Now let me turn to a task that is the primary responsibility of National Government—the safety and security of our people.

Today, we utter no prayer more fervently than the ancient prayer for peace on Earth. Yet history has shown that peace does not come, nor will our freedom be preserved, by good will alone. There are those in the world who scorn our vision of human dignity and freedom. One nation, the Soviet Union, has conducted the greatest military buildup in the history of man, building arsenals of awesome offensive weapons.

We've made progress in restoring our defense capability. But much remains to be done. There must be no wavering by us, nor any doubts by others, that America will meet her responsibilities to remain free, secure, and at peace.

There is only one way safely and legitimately to reduce the cost of national security, and that is to reduce the need for it. And this we're trying to do in negotiations with the Soviet Union. We're not just discussing limits on a further increase of nuclear weapons; we seek, instead, to reduce their number. We seek the total elimination one day of nuclear weapons from the face of the Earth.

Now, for decades, we and the Soviets have lived under the threat of mutual assured destruction—if either resorted to the use of nuclear weapons, the other could retaliate and destroy the one who had started it. Is there either logic or morality in believing that if one side threatens to kill tens of millions of our people our only recourse is to threaten killing tens of millions of theirs? I have approved a research program to find, if we can, a security shield that will destroy nuclear missiles before they reach their target. It wouldn't kill people; it would destroy weapons. It wouldn't militarize space; it would help demilitarize the arsenals of Earth. It would render nuclear weapons obsolete. We will meet with the Soviets, hoping that we can agree on a way to rid the world of the threat of nuclear destruction.

We strive for peace and security, heartened by the changes all around us. Since the turn of the century, the number of democracies in the world has grown fourfold. Human freedom is on the march, and nowhere more so than in our own hemisphere. Freedom is one of the deepest and noblest aspirations of the human spirit. People, worldwide, hunger for the right of self-determination, for those inalienable rights that make for human dignity and progress.

America must remain freedom's staunchest friend, for freedom is our best ally and it is the world's only hope to conquer poverty and preserve peace. Every blow we inflict against poverty will be a blow against its dark allies of oppression and war. Every victory for human freedom will be a victory for world peace.

So, we go forward today, a nation still mighty in its youth and powerful in its purpose. With our alliances strengthened, with our economy leading the world to a new age of economic expansion, we look to a future rich in possibilities. And all of this is because we worked and acted together, not as members of political parties but as Americans.

My friends, we live in a world that's lit by lightning. So much is changing and will change, but so much endures and transcends time.

History is a ribbon, always unfurling. History is a journey. And as we continue our journey, we think of those who traveled before us. We stand again at the steps of this symbol of our democracy—well, we would have been standing at the steps if it hadn't gotten so cold. Now we're standing inside this symbol of our democracy, and we see and hear again the echoes of our past—a general falls to his knees in the hard snow of Valley Forge; a lonely President paces the darkened halls and ponders his struggle to preserve the Union; the men of the Alamo call out encouragement to each other; a settler pushes west and sings a song, and the song echoes out forever and fills the unknowing air.

It is the American sound. It is hopeful, big-hearted, idealistic, daring, decent, and fair. That's our heritage, that's our song. We sing it still. For all our problems, our differences, we are together as of old. We raise our voices to the God who is the Author of this most tender music. And may He continue to hold us close as we fill the world with our sound—in unity, affection, and love—one people under God, dedicated to the dream of freedom that He has placed in the human heart, called upon now to pass that dream on to a waiting and hopeful world.

God bless you, and God bless America.

A Second American Revolution
February 6, 1985

The President shall from time to time give to the Congress information on the State of the Union.

—The United States Constitution

I come before you to report on the state of our Union, and I'm pleased to report that after four years of united effort, the American people have brought forth a nation renewed, stronger, freer, and more secure than before.

Four years ago we began to change, forever I hope, our assumptions about government and its place in our lives. Out of that change has come great and robust growth—in our confidence, our economy, and our role in the world.

Tonight America is stronger because of the values that we hold dear. We believe faith and freedom must be our guiding stars, for they show us truth, they make us brave, give us hope, and leave us wiser than we were. Our progress began not in Washington, DC, but in the hearts of our families, communities, workplaces, and voluntary groups which, together, are unleashing the invincible spirit of one great nation under God.

Four years ago we said we would invigorate our economy by giving people greater freedom and incentives to take risks and letting them keep more of what they earned. We did what we promised, and a great industrial giant is reborn....

New freedom in our lives has planted the rich seeds for future success—for an America of wisdom that honors the family, knowing that if [as] the family goes, so goes our civilization—for an America of vision that sees tomorrow's dreams in the learning and hard work we do today—for an America of courage whose service men and women, even as we meet, proudly stand watch on the frontiers of freedom—for an America of compassion that opens its heart to those who cry out for help.

We have begun well. But it's only a beginning. We're not here to congratulate ourselves on what we have done but to challenge ourselves to finish what has not yet been done.

We're here to speak for millions in our inner cities who long for real jobs, safe neighborhoods, and schools that truly teach. We're here to speak for the American farmer, the entrepreneur, and every worker in industries fighting to modernize and compete. And, yes, we're here to stand, and proudly so, for all who struggle to break free from totalitarianism, for all who know in their hearts that freedom is the one true path to peace and human happiness.

Proverbs tells us, without a vision the people perish. When asked what great principle holds our Union together, Abraham Lincoln said, "Something in the Declaration [of Independence] giving liberty, not alone to the people of this country, but hope to the world for all future time."

We honor the giants of our history not by going back but forward to the dreams their vision foresaw. My fellow citizens, this nation is poised for greatness. The time has come to proceed toward a great new challenge—a second American Revolution of hope and opportunity; a revolution carrying us to new heights of progress by pushing back frontiers of knowledge and space; a revolution of spirit that taps the soul of America, enabling us to summon greater strength than we've ever known; and a revolution that carries beyond our shores the golden promise of human freedom in a world of peace.

Let us begin by challenging our conventional wisdom. There are no constraints on the human mind, no walls around the human spirit, no barriers to our progress except those we ourselves erect. Already, pushing down tax rates has freed our economy to vault forward to record growth.

In Europe, they're calling it "the American Miracle." Day by day, we're shattering accepted notions of what is possible. When I was growing up, we failed to see how a new thing called radio would transform our marketplace. Well, today, many have not yet seen how advances in technology are transforming our lives....

We stand on the threshold of a great ability to produce more, do more, be more. Our economy is not getting older and weaker; it's getting younger and stronger. It doesn't need rest and supervision; it needs new challenge, greater freedom. And that word "freedom" is the key to the second American revolution that we need to bring about....

Now, there's another great heritage to speak of this evening. Of all the changes that have swept America the past four years, none brings greater promise than our rediscovery of the values of faith, freedom, family, work, and neighborhood. We see signs of renewal in increased attendance in places of worship; renewed optimism and faith in our future; love of country rediscovered by our young, who are leading the way. We've rediscovered that work is good in and of itself, that it ennobles us to create and contribute no matter how seemingly humble our jobs. We've seen a powerful new current from an old and honorable tradition—American generosity....

For the past twenty years we've believed that no war will be launched as long as each side knows it can retaliate with a deadly counterstrike. Well, I believe there's a better way of eliminating the threat of nuclear war. It is a Strategic Defense Initiative aimed ultimately at finding a nonnuclear defense against ballistic missiles. It's the most hopeful possibility of the nuclear age. But it's not very well understood. Some say it will bring war to the heavens, but its purpose is to deter war in the heavens and on Earth. Now, some say the research would be expensive. Perhaps, but it could save millions of lives, indeed humanity itself. And some say if we build such a system, the Soviets will build a defense system of their own. Well, they already have strategic defenses that surpass ours; a civil defense system, where we have almost none; and a research program covering roughly the same areas of technology that we're now exploring. And finally some say the research will take a long time. Well, the answer to that is: "Let's get started."

Harry Truman once said that, ultimately, our security and the world's hopes for peace and human progress "lie not in measures of defense or in the control of weapons, but in the growth and expansion of freedom and self-government."

And tonight, we declare anew to our fellow citizens of the world: Freedom is not the sole prerogative of a chosen few; it is the universal right of all God's children. Look to where peace and prosperity flourish today. It is in homes that freedom built. Victories against poverty are greatest and peace most secure where people live by laws that ensure free press, free speech, and freedom to worship, vote, and create wealth.... We cannot play innocents abroad in a world that's not innocent; nor can we be passive when freedom is under siege....

Tonight, I've spoken of great plans and great dreams. They're dreams we can make come true. Two hundred years of American history should have taught us that nothing is impossible.

Ten years ago a young girl left Vietnam with her family, part of the exodus that followed the fall of Saigon. They came to the United States with no possessions and not knowing a word of English. Ten years ago—the young girl studied hard, learned English, and finished high school in the top of her class. And this May, May 22d to be exact, is a big date on her calendar. Just 10 years from the time she left Vietnam, she will graduate from the United States Military Academy at West Point. I thought you might like to meet an American hero named Jean Nguyen.

Now, there's someone else here tonight, born seventy-nine years ago. She lives in the inner city, where she cares for infants born of mothers who are heroin addicts. The children, born in withdrawal, are sometimes even dropped on her doorstep. She helps them with love. Go to her house some night, and maybe you'll see her silhouette against the window as she walks the floor talking softly, soothing a child in her arms—Mother Hale of Harlem, and she, too, is an American hero.

Jean, Mother Hale, your lives tell us that the oldest American saying is new again: Anything is possible in America if we have the faith, the will, and the heart. History is asking us once again to be a force for good in the world. Let us begin in unity, with justice, and love.

Thank you, and God bless you.

There's Work To Do
March 8, 1985

Governor Reagan's speech to the Conservative Political Action Conference.

.... I've been thinking, in the weeks since the inauguration, that we are at an especially dramatic turning point in American history. And just putting it all together in my mind, I've been reviewing the elements that have led to this moment.

Ever since F.D.R. and the New Deal, the opposition party, and particularly those of a liberal persuasion, have dominated the political debate. Their ideas were new; they had momentum; they captured the imagination of the American people. The left held sway for a good long time. There was a right, but it was, by the '40s and '50s, diffuse and scattered, without a unifying voice.

But in 1964 came a voice in the wilderness—Barry Goldwater; the great Barry Goldwater, the first major party candidate of our time who was a true-blue, undiluted conservative. He spoke from principle, and he offered vision. Freedom—he spoke of freedom: freedom from the Government's increasing demands on the family purse, freedom from the Government's increasing usurpation of individual rights and responsibilities, freedom from the leaders who told us the price of world peace is continued acquiescence to totalitarianism. He was ahead of his time. When he ran for President, he won six states and lost forty-four. But his candidacy worked as a precursor of things to come.

A new movement was stirring. And in the 1960's Young Americans for Freedom is born; *National Review* gains readership and prestige in the intellectual community; *Human Events* becomes a major voice on the cutting edge. In the '70s the anti-tax movement begins. Actually, it was much more than an anti-tax movement, just as the Boston Tea Party was much more than anti-tax initiative. In the late '70s Proposition 13 and the Sagebrush Rebellion; in 1980, for the first time in twenty-eight years, a Republican Senate is elected; so, may I say, is a conservative President. In 1984 that conservative administration is reelected in a forty-nine state sweep. And the day the votes came in, I thought of Walt Whitman: "I hear America singing."

This great turn from left to right was not just a case of the pendulum swinging. First, the left hold sway and then the right, and here comes the left again. The truth is, conservative thought is no longer over here on the right; it's the mainstream now. And the tide of history is moving irresistibly in our direction. Why? Because the other side is virtually bankrupt of ideas. It has nothing more to say, nothing to add to the debate. It has spent its intellectual capital, such as it was, and it has done its deeds. Now, we're not in power now because they failed to gain electoral support over the past 50 years. They did win support. And the result was chaos, weakness, and drift. Ultimately, though, their failures yielded one great thing—us guys. We in this room are not simply profiting from their bankruptcy; we are where we are because we're winning the contest of ideas. In fact, in the past decade, all of a sudden, quietly, mysteriously, the Republican Party has become the party of ideas.

We became the party of the most brilliant and dynamic young minds. I remember them, just a few years ago, running around scrawling Laffer curves on table napkins, going to symposia and talking about how social programs did not eradicate poverty, but entrenched it; writing studies on why the latest weird and unnatural idea from the social engineers is weird and unnatural. You were there. They were your ideas, your symposia, your books, and usually somebody else's table napkins.

All of a sudden, Republicans were not defenders of the status quo but creators of the future. They were looking at tomorrow with all the single-mindedness of an inventor. In fact, they reminded me of the American inventors of the 19th and 20th centuries who filled the world with light and recorded sound.

The new conservatives made anew the connection between economic justice and economic growth. Growth in the economy would not only create jobs and paychecks, they said; it would enhance familial stability and encourage a healthy optimism about the future. Lower those tax rates, they said, and let the economy become the engine of our dreams. Pull back regulations, and encourage free and open competition. Let the men and women of the marketplace decide what they want.

But along with that, perhaps the greatest triumph of modern conservatism has been to stop allowing the left to put the average

American on the moral defensive. By average American I mean the good, decent, rambunctious, and creative people who raise the families, go to church, and help out when the local library holds a fundraiser; people who have a stake in the community because they are the community.

These people had held true to certain beliefs and principles that for 20 years the intelligentsia were telling us were hopelessly out of date, utterly trite, and reactionary. You want prayer in the schools? How primitive, they said. You oppose abortion? How oppressive, how antimodern. The normal was portrayed as eccentric, and only the abnormal was worthy of emulation. The irreverent was celebrated, but only irreverence about certain things: irreverence toward, say, organized religion, yes; irreverence toward establishment liberalism, not too much of that. They celebrated their courage in taking on safe targets and patted each other on the back for slinging stones at a confused Goliath, who was too demoralized and really too good to fight back. But now one simply senses it. The American people are no longer on the defensive. I believe the conservative movement deserves some credit for this. You spoke for the permanent against the merely prevalent, and ultimately you prevailed.

I believe we conservatives have captured the moment, captured the imagination of the American people. And what now? What are we to do with our success? Well, right now, with conservative thought accepted as mainstream thought and with the people of our country leading the fight to freedom, now we must move.

You remember your Shakespeare: "There is a tide in the affairs of men which, taken at the flood, leads on to fortune. Omitted, all the voyage of their life is bound in shallows and in miseries. On such a full sea are we now afloat. And we must take the current when it serves, or lose our ventures."

.... I spoke in the State of the Union of a second American revolution, and now is the time to launch that revolution and see that it takes hold. If we move decisively, these years will not be just a passing era of good feeling, not just a few good years, but a true golden age of freedom. The moment is ours, and we must seize it. There's work to do!

.... Once during the campaign, I said, "This is a wonderful time to be alive." And I meant that. I meant that we're lucky not to live in pale and timid times. We've been blessed with the opportunity to stand for something—for liberty and freedom and fairness. And these are things worth fighting for, worth devoting our lives to. And we have good reason to be hopeful and optimistic.

We've made much progress already. So, let us go forth with good cheer and stout hearts—happy warriors out to seize back a country and a world to freedom.

Thank you, and God bless you. Thank you very much.

Terrorism
July 8, 1985

President Reagan's speech on the threats to America from terrorist states.

.... There is a temptation to see the terrorist act as simply the erratic work of a small group of fanatics. We make this mistake at great peril, for the attacks on America, her citizens, her allies, and other democratic nations in recent years do form a pattern of terrorism that has strategic implications and political goals. And only by moving our focus from the tactical to the strategic perspective, only by identifying the pattern of terror and those behind it, can we hope to put into force a strategy to deal with it.

.... Iran, Libya, North Korea, Cuba, Nicaragua—continents away, tens of thousands of miles apart, but the same goals and objectives. I submit to you that the growth in terrorism in recent years results from the increasing involvement of these states in terrorism in every region of the world. This is terrorism that is part of a pattern, the work of a confederation of terrorist states. Most of the terrorists who are kidnaping and murdering American citizens and attacking American installations are being trained, financed, and directly or indirectly controlled by a core group of radical and totalitarian governments—a new, international version of Murder, Incorporated. And all of these states are united by one simple criminal phenomenon—their fanatical hatred of the United States, our people, our way of life, our international stature.

And the strategic purpose behind the terrorism sponsored by these outlaw states is clear: to disorient the United States, to disrupt or alter our foreign policy, to sow discord between ourselves and our allies, to frighten friendly Third World nations working with us for peaceful settlements of regional conflicts, and, finally, to remove American influence from those areas of the world where we're working to bring stable and democratic government; in short, to cause us to retreat, retrench, to become Fortress America.

Yes, their real goal is to expel America from the world. And that is the reason these terrorist nations are arming, training, and supporting attacks against this nation. And that is why we can be clear on one point—these terrorist states are now engaged in acts of war against the Government and people of the United States. And under international law, any state which is the victim of acts of war has the right to defend itself.

Now, for the benefit of these outlaw governments who are sponsoring international terrorism against our nation, I'm prepared to offer a brief lesson in American history. A number of times in America's past, foreign tyrants, warlords, and totalitarian dictators have misinterpreted the well-known likeability, patience, and generosity of the American people as signs of weakness or even decadence. Well, it's true; we are an easygoing people, slow to wrath, hesitant to see danger looming over every horizon. But it's also true that when the emotions of the American people are aroused, when their patriotism and their anger are triggered, there are no limits to their national valor nor their consuming passion to protect this nation's cherished tradition of freedom. Teddy Roosevelt once put it this way: "The American people are slow to wrath, but when the wrath is once kindled it burns like a consuming flame." And it was another leader, this time a foreign adversary, Admiral Yamamoto, who warned his own nation after its attack on Pearl Harbor that he feared "we have only awakened a sleeping giant and his reaction will be terrible."

Yes, we Americans have our disagreements, sometimes noisy ones, almost always in public—that's the nature of our open society—but no foreign power should mistake disagreement for disunity. Those who are tempted to do so should reflect on our national character and our history—a history littered with the wreckage of regimes who made the mistake of underestimating the vigor and will of the American people.

So, let me today speak for a united people. Let me say simply: We're Americans. We love this country. We love what she stands for, and we will always defend her. We live for freedom—our own, our children's—and we will always stand ready to sacrifice for that freedom.

So, the American people are not—I repeat not—going to tolerate intimidation, terror, and outright acts of war against this nation and its people. And we're especially not going to tolerate these attacks from outlaw states run by the strangest collection of misfits, loony tunes, and squalid criminals since the advent of the Third Reich.

Now, I've taken your time today to outline the nature of this network of terrorist states so that we might, as a nation, know who it is we're up against and identify the long-term goals motivating this confederation of criminal governments. Do not for a moment, however, think that this discussion has been all inclusive. First of all, though their strength does not match that of the groups supported by the terrorist network I've already mentioned, there are some terrorist organizations that are indigenous to certain localities or countries which are not necessarily tied to this international network. And second, the countries I have mentioned today are not necessarily the only ones that support terrorism against the United States and its allies. Those which I've described are simply the ones that can be most directly implicated.

.... Now, much needs to be done by all of us in the community of civilized nations. We must act against the criminal menace of terrorism with the full weight of the law, both domestic and international. We will act to indict, apprehend, and prosecute those who commit the kind of atrocities the world has witnessed in recent weeks. We can act together as free peoples who wish not to see our citizens kidnapped or shot or blown out of the skies—just as we acted together to rid the seas of piracy at the turn of the last century. And incidentally, those of you who are legal scholars will note the law's description of pirates—"hostis humanis" —the enemies of all mankind. There can be no place on Earth left where it is safe for these monsters to rest or train or practice their cruel and deadly skills. We must act together, or unilaterally if necessary, to ensure that terrorists have no sanctuary anywhere.

.... Finally, I want you to accept a challenge to become part of the solution to the problem of terrorism. You have a fundamental concern for the law, and it's upon the law that terrorists trample. You need to address this problem in conferences and conventions that will lead us to a better domestic and international legal framework for dealing with terrorism. You must help this government and others to deal legally with lawlessness. Where legislation must be crafted to allow appropriate authorities to act, you should help to craft or change it. In the past lawyers have helped when civilization was threatened by lawbreakers, and now is the time to do so again.

What I place before you this morning is not pleasant, nor will the solution be easy. The answer to the threat of international terrorism is difficult, but it can be found. It is to be found in a clear understanding of the problem and the expression of our national will to do something about it. It's always been so with any important cause; it's why our Declaration of Independence was more important to our Revolution than any one military maneuver or single battle. And that is why we do not today engage in policy discussions or focus on strategic options but simply state the facts about the nature of international terrorism and affirm America's will to resist it.

But there's another point that needs to be made here, the point I made at the start of this discussion: that in taking a strategic—not just a tactical—view of terrorism, we must understand that the greatest hope the terrorists and their supporters harbor, the very reason for their cruelty and viciousness of their tactics, is to disorient the American people, to cause disunity, to disrupt or alter our foreign policy, to keep us from the steady pursuit of our strategic interests, to distract us from our very real hope that someday the nightmare of totalitarian rule will end and self-government and personal freedom will become the birthright of every people on Earth.

And here, my fellow Americans, is where we find the real motive behind the rabid and increasing anti-Americanism of the international terrorist network. I've been saying for some years now that the cause of totalitarian ideology is on the wane; that all across the world there is an uprising of mind and will, a tidal wave of longing for freedom and self-rule. Well, no one senses this better than those who now stand atop totalitarian states, especially those nations on the outer periphery of the totalitarian world like Iran, Libya, North Korea, Cuba, and Nicaragua. Their rulers are frightened; they know that freedom is on the march and when it triumphs their time in power is over.

You see, it's true that totalitarian governments are very powerful and, over the short term, may be better organized than the democracies. But it's also true—and no one knows this better than totalitarian rulers themselves—that these regimes are weak in a way that no democracy can ever be weak. For the fragility of totalitarian government is the fragility of any regime whose hold on its people is limited to the instruments of police-state repression. That's why the stakes are so high and why we must persevere. Freedom itself is the issue—our own and the entire world's. Yes, America is still a symbol to a few, a symbol that is feared and hated, but to more, many millions more, a symbol that is loved, a country that remains a shining city on a hill.

Teddy Roosevelt—and he is a good President to quote in these circumstances—put it so well: "We, here in America, hold in our hands the hope of the world, the fate of the coming years; and shame and disgrace will be ours if in our eyes the light of high resolve is dimmed, if we trail in the dust the golden hopes of man." And that light of high resolve, those golden hopes, are now ours to preserve and protect and, with God's help, to pass on to generations to come....

Thank you very much. God bless you all.

The Challenger Disaster
January 28, 1986

On January 28, 1986 the space shuttle Challenger, carrying a crew of seven, including the first schoolteacher in space, Christa McAuliffe, exploded over the Kennedy Space Center. President Reagan addressed the nation.

Ladies and Gentlemen, I'd planned to speak to you tonight to report on the state of the Union, but the events of earlier today have led me to change those plans. Today is a day for mourning and remembering. Nancy and I are pained to the core by the tragedy of the shuttle Challenger. We know we share this pain with all of the people of our country. This is truly a national loss.

Nineteen years ago, almost to the day, we lost three astronauts in a terrible accident on the ground. But we've never lost an astronaut in flight; we've never had a tragedy like this. And perhaps we've forgotten the courage it took for the crew of the shuttle. But they, the Challenger Seven, were aware of the dangers, but overcame them and did their jobs brilliantly. We mourn seven heroes: Michael Smith, Dick Scobee, Judith Resnik, Ronald McNair, Ellison Onizuka, Gregory Jarvis, and Christa McAuliffe. We mourn their loss as a nation together.

For the families of the seven, we cannot bear, as you do, the full impact of this tragedy. But we feel the loss, and we're thinking about you so very much. Your loved ones were daring and brave, and they had that special grace, that special spirit that says, "Give me a challenge, and I'll meet it with joy." They had a hunger to explore the universe and discover its truths. They wished to serve, and they did. They served all of us.

We've grown used to wonders in this century. It's hard to dazzle us. But for twenty-five years the United States space program has been doing just that. We've grown used to the idea of space, and perhaps we forget that we've only just begun. We're still pioneers. They, the members of the Challenger crew, were pioneers.

And I want to say something to the schoolchildren of America who were watching the live coverage of the shuttle's takeoff. I know it is hard to understand, but sometimes painful things like this happen. It's all part of the process of exploration and discovery. It's all part of taking a chance and expanding man's horizons. The future doesn't belong to the fainthearted; it belongs to the brave. The Challenger crew was pulling us into the future, and we'll continue to follow them.

I've always had great faith in and respect for our space program, and what happened today does nothing to diminish it. We don't hide our space program. We don't keep secrets and cover things up. We do it all up front and in public. That's the way freedom is, and we wouldn't change it for a minute. We'll continue our quest in space. There will be more shuttle flights and more shuttle crews and, yes, more volunteers, more civilians, more teachers in space. Nothing ends here; our hopes and our journeys continue. I want to add that I wish I could talk to every man and woman who works for NASA or who worked on this mission and tell them: "Your dedication and professionalism have moved and impressed us for decades. And we know of your anguish. We share it."

There's a coincidence today. On this day 390 years ago, the great explorer Sir Francis Drake died aboard ship off the coast of Panama. In his lifetime the great frontiers were the oceans, and an historian later said, "He lived by the sea, died on it, and was buried in it." Well, today we can say of the Challenger crew: Their dedication was, like Drake's, complete.

The crew of the space shuttle Challenger honored us by the manner in which they lived their lives. We will never forget them, nor the last time we saw them, this morning, as they prepared for their journey and waved goodbye and "slipped the surly bonds of earth" to "touch the face of God."

The American Dream
February 4, 1986

The President shall from time to time give to the Congress information on the State of the Union.

—The United States Constitution

Mr. Speaker, Mr. President, distinguished Members of the Congress, honored guests, and fellow citizens, thank you for allowing me to delay my address until this evening. We paused together to mourn and honor the valor of our seven Challenger heroes. And I hope that we are now ready to do what they would want us to do—go forward, America, and reach for the stars. We will never forget those brave seven, but we shall go forward....

I have come to review with you the progress of our nation, to speak of unfinished work, and to set our sights on the future. I am pleased to report the state of our Union is stronger than a year ago and growing stronger each day. Tonight we look out on a rising America—firm of heart, united in spirit, powerful in pride and patriotism. America is on the move!

But it wasn't long ago that we looked out on a different land: locked factory gates, long gasoline lines, intolerable prices, and interest rates turning the greatest country on Earth into a land of broken dreams. Government growing beyond our consent had become a lumbering giant, slamming shut the gates of opportunity, threatening to crush the very roots of our freedom.

What brought America back? The American people brought us back—with quiet courage and common sense, with undying faith that in this nation under God the future will be ours; for the future belongs to the free....

And despite the pressures of our modern world, family and community remain the moral core of our society, guardians of our values and hopes for the future. Family and community are the costars of this great American comeback. They are why we say tonight: Private values must be at the heart of public policies.

What is true for families in America is true for America in the family of free nations. History is no captive of some inevitable force. History is made by men and women of vision and courage. Tonight freedom is on the march. The United States is the economic miracle, the model to which the world once again turns. We stand for an idea whose time is now: Only by lifting the weights from the shoulders of all can people truly prosper and can peace among all nations be secure.

Teddy Roosevelt said that a nation that does great work lives forever. We have done well, but we cannot stop at the foothills when Everest beckons. It's time for America to be all that we can be....

How often we read of a husband and wife both working, struggling from paycheck to paycheck to raise a family, meet a mortgage, pay their taxes and bills. And yet some in Congress say taxes must be raised. Well, I'm sorry—they're asking the wrong people to tighten their belts. It's time we reduce the Federal budget and left the family budget alone. We do not face large deficits because American families are undertaxed; we face those deficits because the Federal Government overspends....

Keeping America strong is as vital to the national security as controlling Federal spending is to our economic security. But, as I have said before, the most powerful force we can enlist against the Federal deficit is an ever-expanding American economy, unfettered and free.

The magic of opportunity—unreserved, unfailing, unrestrained—isn't this the calling that unites us? I believe our tax rate cuts for the people have done more to spur a spirit of risk-taking and help America's economy break free than any program since John Kennedy's tax cut almost a quarter century ago.

Now history calls us to press on, to complete efforts for an historic tax reform providing new opportunity for all and ensuring that all pay their fair share—but no more. We've come this far. Will you join me now, and we'll walk this last mile together?

.... As we work to make the American dream real for all, we must also look to the condition of America's families. Struggling parents today worry how they will provide their children the advantages that their parents gave them. In the welfare culture, the breakdown of the family, the most basic support system, has reached crisis proportions—in female and child poverty, child abandonment, horrible crimes, and deteriorating schools. After hundreds of billions of dollars in poverty programs, the plight of the poor grows more painful. But the waste in dollars and cents pales before the most tragic loss—the sinful waste of human spirit and potential.

We can ignore this terrible truth no longer. As Franklin Roosevelt warned fifty-one years ago, standing before this Chamber, he said, "Welfare is a narcotic, a subtle destroyer of the human spirit." And we must now escape the spider's web of dependency. Tonight I am charging the White House Domestic Council to present me by December 1, 1986, an evaluation of programs and a strategy for immediate action to meet the financial, educational, social, and safety concerns of poor families. I'm talking about real and lasting emancipation, because the success of welfare should be judged by how many of its recipients become independent of welfare....

And tonight I want to speak directly to America's younger generation, because you hold the destiny of our nation in your hands. With all the temptations young people face, it sometimes seems the allure of the permissive society requires superhuman feats of self-control. But the call of the future is too strong, the challenge too great to get lost in the blind alleyways of dissolution, drugs, and despair. Never has there been a more exciting time to be alive—a time of rousing wonder and heroic achievement. As they said in the film *Back to the Future*, "Where we're going, we don't need roads."

.... What we accomplish this year, in each challenge we face, will set our course for the balance of the decade, indeed, for the remainder of the century. After all we've done so far, let no one say that this nation cannot reach the destiny of our dreams. America believes, America is ready, America can win the race to the future—and we shall. The American dream is a song of hope that rings through night winter air; vivid, tender music that warms our hearts when the least among us aspire to the greatest things—to venture a daring enterprise; to unearth new beauty in music, literature, and art; to discover a new universe inside a tiny silicon chip or a single human cell.

We see the dream coming true in the spirit of discovery of Richard Cavoli—all his life he's been enthralled by the mysteries of medicine. And, Richard, we know that the experiment that you began in high school was launched and lost last week, yet your dream lives. And as long as it's real, work of noble note will yet be done—work that could reduce the harmful effects of x-rays on patients and enable astronomers to view the golden gateways of the farthest stars.

We see the dream glow in the towering talent of a twelve-year-old, Tyrone Ford—a child prodigy of gospel music, he has surmounted personal adversity to become an accomplished pianist and singer. He also directs the choirs of three churches and has performed at the Kennedy Center. With God as your composer, Tyrone, your music will be the music of angels.

We see the dream being saved by the courage of the thirteen-year-old Shelby Butler—honor student and member of her school's safety patrol. Seeing another girl freeze in terror before an out-of-control school bus, she risked her life and pulled her to safety. With bravery like yours, Shelby, America need never fear for our future.

And we see the dream born again in the joyful compassion of a thirteen-year-old, Trevor Ferrell. Two years ago, age eleven, watching men and women bedding down in abandoned doorways—on television he was watching—Trevor left his suburban Philadelphia home to bring blankets and food to the helpless and homeless. And now 250 people help him fulfill his nightly vigil. Trevor, yours is the living spirit of brotherly love. Would you four stand up for a moment?

Thank you, thank you. You are heroes of our hearts. We look at you and know it's true—in this land of dreams fulfilled, where greater dreams may be imagined, nothing is impossible, no victory is beyond our reach, no glory will ever be too great.

So, now it's up to us, all of us, to prepare America for that day when our work will pale before the greatness of America's champions in the 21st century. The world's hopes rest with America's future; America's hopes rest with us. So, let us go forward to create our world of tomorrow in faith, in unity, and in love.

God bless you and God bless America.

Just Say No!
September 14, 1986

The President and Mrs. Reagan spoke to the nation on the problem of drug addiction, urging America's children to "Just Say No!"

Good evening. Usually, I talk with you from my office in the West Wing of the White House. But tonight there's something special to talk about, and I've asked someone very special to join me. Nancy and I are here in the West Hall of the White House, and around us are the rooms in which we live. It's the home you've provided for us, of which we merely have temporary custody.

Nancy's joining me because the message this evening is not my message but ours. And we speak to you not simply as fellow citizens but as fellow parents and grandparents and as concerned neighbors. It's back-to-school time for America's children. And while drug and alcohol abuse cuts across all generations, it's especially damaging to the young people on whom our future depends. So tonight, from our family to yours, from our home to yours, thank you for joining us.

America has accomplished so much in these last few years, whether it's been rebuilding our economy or serving the cause of freedom in the world. What we've been able to achieve has been done with your help—with us working together as a nation united. Now, we need your support again. Drugs are menacing our society. They're threatening our values and undercutting our institutions. They're killing our children.... Despite our best efforts, illegal cocaine is coming into our country at alarming levels, and four to five million people regularly use it. Five hundred thousand Americans are hooked on heroin. One in twelve persons smokes marijuana regularly. Regular drug use is even higher among the age group 18 to 25, most likely just entering the workforce. Today there's a new epidemic: smokable cocaine, otherwise known as crack. It is an explosively destructive and often lethal substance which is crushing its users. It is an uncontrolled fire. And drug abuse is not a so-called victimless crime. Everyone's safety is at stake when drugs and excessive alcohol are used by people on the highways or by those transporting our citizens or operating industrial equipment. Drug abuse costs you and your fellow Americans at least $60 billion a year.

From the early days of our administration, Nancy has been intensely involved in the effort to fight drug abuse. She has since traveled over 100,000 miles to fifty-five cities in twenty-eight States and six foreign countries to fight school-age drug and alcohol abuse. She's given dozens of speeches and scores of interviews and has participated in twenty-four special radio and TV tapings to create greater awareness of this crisis. Her personal observations and efforts have given her such dramatic insights that I wanted her to share them with you this evening.

Mrs. Reagan: Thank you. As a mother, I've always thought of September as a special month, a time when we bundled our children off to school, to the warmth of an environment in which they could fulfill the promise and hope in those restless minds. But so much has happened over these last years, so much to shake the foundations of all that we know and all that we believe in. Today there's a drug and alcohol abuse epidemic in this country, and no one is safe from it—not you, not me, and certainly not our children, because this epidemic has their names written on it. Many of you may be thinking: "Well, drugs don't concern me." But it does concern you. It concerns us all because of the way it tears at our lives and because it's aimed at destroying the brightness and life of the sons and daughters of the United States.

For five years I've been traveling across the country, learning and listening. And one of the most hopeful signs I've seen is the building of an essential, new awareness of how terrible and threatening drug abuse is to our society. This was one of the main purposes when I started, so of course it makes me happy that that's been accomplished. But each time I meet with someone new or receive another letter from a troubled person on drugs, I yearn to find a way to help share the message that cries out from them. As a parent, I'm especially concerned about what drugs are doing to young mothers and their newborn children. Listen to this news account from a hospital in Florida of a child born to a mother with a cocaine habit: "Nearby, a baby named Paul lies motionless in an incubator, feeding tubes riddling his tiny body. He needs a respirator to breathe and a daily spinal tap to relieve fluid buildup on his brain. Only 1 month old, he's already suffered 2 strokes."

Now you can see why drug abuse concerns every one of us—all the American family. Drugs steal away so much. They take and take, until finally every time a drug goes into a child, something else is forced out, like love and hope and trust and confidence. Drugs take away the dream from every child's heart and replace it with a nightmare, and it's time we in America stand up and replace those dreams. Each of us has to put our principles and consciences on the line, whether in social settings or in the workplace, to set forth solid standards and stick to them. There's no moral middle ground. Indifference is not an option. We want you to help us create an outspoken intolerance for drug use. For the sake of our children, I implore each of you to be unyielding and inflexible in your opposition to drugs.

Our young people are helping us lead the way. Not long ago, in Oakland, California, I was asked by a group of children what to do if they were offered drugs, and I answered, "Just say no." Soon after that, those children in Oakland formed a Just Say No club, and now there are over 10,000 such clubs all over the country. Well, their participation and their courage in saying no needs our encouragement. We can help by using every opportunity to force the issue of not using drugs to the point of making others uncomfortable, even if it means making ourselves unpopular.

Our job is never easy because drug criminals are ingenious. They work everyday to plot a new and better way to steal our children's lives, just as they've done by developing this new drug, crack. For every door that we close, they open a new door to death. They prosper on our unwillingness to act. So, we must be smarter and stronger and tougher than they are. It's up to us to change attitudes and just simply dry up their markets.

And finally, to young people watching or listening, I have a very personal message for you: There's a big, wonderful world out there for you. It belongs to you. It's exciting and stimulating and rewarding. Don't cheat yourselves out of this promise. Our country needs you, but it needs you to be clear-eyed and clear-minded. I recently read one teenager's story. She's now determined to stay clean but was once strung out on several drugs. What she remembered most clearly about her recovery was that during the time she was on drugs everything appeared to her in shades of black and gray and after her treatment she was able to see colors again.

So, to my young friends out there: Life can be great, but not when you can't see it. So, open your eyes to life: to see it in the vivid colors that God gave us as a precious gift to His children, to enjoy life to the fullest, and to make it count. Say yes to your life. And when it comes to drugs and alcohol just say no.

President Reagan: I think you can see why Nancy has been such a positive influence on all that we're trying to do. The job ahead of us is very clear. Nancy's personal crusade, like that of so many other wonderful individuals, should become our national crusade. It must include a combination of government and private efforts which complement one another. Last month I announced six initiatives which we believe will do just that.

First, we seek a drug-free workplace at all levels of government and in the private sector. Second, we'll work toward drug-free schools. Third, we want to ensure that the public is protected and that treatment is available to substance abusers and the chemically dependent. Our fourth goal is to expand international cooperation while treating drug trafficking as a threat to our national security. In October I will be meeting with key U.S. Ambassadors to discuss what can be done to support our friends abroad. Fifth, we must move to strengthen law enforcement activities such as those initiated by Vice President Bush and Attorney General Meese. And finally, we seek to expand public awareness and prevention.

In order to further implement these six goals, I will announce tomorrow a series of new proposals for a drug-free America. Taken as a whole, these proposals will toughen our laws against drug criminals, encourage more research and treatment, and ensure that illegal drugs will not be tolerated in our schools or in our workplaces. Together with our ongoing efforts, these proposals will bring the Federal commitment to fighting drugs to $3 billion. As much financing as we commit, however, we would be fooling ourselves if we thought that massive new amounts of money alone will provide the solution. Let us not forget that in America people solve problems and no national crusade has ever succeeded without human investment. Winning the crusade against drugs will not be achieved by just throwing money at the problem. Your government will continue to act aggressively, but nothing would be more effective than for Americans simply to quit using illegal drugs. We seek to create a massive change in national attitudes which ultimately will separate the drugs from the customer, to take the user away from the supply. I believe, quite simply, that we can help them quit, and that's where you come in.

My generation will remember how America swung into action when we were attacked in World War II. The war was not just fought by the fellows flying the planes or driving the tanks. It was fought at home by a mobilized nation—men and women alike—building planes and ships, clothing sailors and soldiers, feeding marines and airmen; and it was fought by children planting victory gardens and collecting cans. Well, now we're in another war for our freedom, and it's time for all of us to pull together again. So, for example, if your friend or neighbor or a family member has a drug or alcohol problem, don't turn the other way. Go to his help or to hers. Get others involved with you—clubs, service groups, and community organizations—and provide support and strength. And, of course, many of you've been cured through treatment and self-help. Well, you're the combat veterans, and you have a critical role to play. You can help others by telling your story and providing a willing hand to those in need. Being friends to others is the best way of being friends to ourselves. It's time, as Nancy said, for America to "Just Say No" to drugs.

Those of you in union halls and workplaces everywhere: Please make this challenge a part of your job every day. Help us preserve the health and dignity of all workers. To businesses large and small: We need the creativity of your enterprise applied directly to this national problem. Help us. And those of you who are educators: Your wisdom and leadership are indispensable to this cause. From the pulpits of this spirit-filled land: We would welcome your reassuring message of redemption and forgiveness and of helping one another. On the athletic fields: You men and women are among the most beloved citizens of our country. A child's eyes fill with your heroic achievements. Few of us can give youngsters something as special and strong to look up to as you. Please don't let them down.

And this camera in front of us: It's a reminder that in Nancy's and my former profession and in the newsrooms and production rooms of our media centers—you have a special opportunity with your enormous influence to send alarm signals across the Nation. To our friends in foreign countries: We know many of you are involved in this battle with us. We need your success as well as ours. When we all come together, united, striving for this cause, then those who are killing America and terrorizing it with slow but sure chemical destruction will see that they are up against the mightiest force for good that we know. Then they will have no dark alleyways to hide in.

In this crusade, let us not forget who we are. Drug abuse is a repudiation of everything America is. The destructiveness and human wreckage mock our heritage. Think for a moment how special it is to be an American. Can we doubt that only a divine providence placed this land, this island of freedom, here as a refuge for all those people on the world who yearn to breathe free? The revolution out of which our liberty was conceived signaled an historical call to an entire world seeking hope. Each new arrival of immigrants rode the crest of that hope. They came, millions seeking a safe harbor from the oppression of cruel regimes. They came, to escape starvation and disease. They came, those surviving the Holocaust and the Soviet gulags. They came, the boat people, chancing death for even a glimmer of hope that they could have a new life. They all came to taste the air redolent and rich with the freedom that is ours. What an insult it will be to what we are and whence we came if we do not rise up together in defiance against this cancer of drugs.

And there's one more thing. The freedom that so many seek in our land has not been preserved without a price. Nancy and I shared that remembrance two years ago at the Normandy American Cemetery in France. In the still of that June afternoon, we walked together among the soldiers of freedom, past the hundreds of white markers which are monuments to courage and memorials to sacrifice. Too many of these and other such graves are the final resting places of teenagers who became men in the roar of battle.

Look what they gave to us who live. Never would they see another sunlit day glistening off a lake or river back home or miles of corn pushing up against the open sky of our plains. The pristine air of our mountains and the driving energy of our cities are theirs no more. Nor would they ever again be a son to their parents or a father to their own children. They did this for you, for me, for a new generation to carry our democratic experiment proudly forward. Well, that's something I think we're obliged to honor, because what they did for us means that we owe as a simple act of civic stewardship to use our freedom wisely for the common good.

As we mobilize for this national crusade, I'm mindful that drugs are a constant temptation for millions. Please remember this when your courage is tested: You are Americans. You're the product of the freest society mankind has ever known. No one, ever, has the right to destroy your dreams and shatter your life.

Right down the end of this hall is the Lincoln Bedroom. But in the Civil War that room was the one President Lincoln used as his office. Memory fills that room, and more than anything that memory drives us to see vividly what President Lincoln sought to save. Above all, it is that America must stand for something and that our heritage lets us stand with a strength of character made more steely by each layer of challenge pressed upon the Nation. We Americans have never been morally neutral against any form of tyranny. Tonight we're asking no more than that we honor what we have been and what we are by standing together.

Now we go on to the next stop: making a final commitment not to tolerate drugs by anyone, anytime, anyplace. So, won't you join us in this great, new national crusade? God bless you, and good night.

We The People
January 27, 1987

The President shall from time to time give to the Congress information on the State of the Union.

—The United States Constitution

Thank you very much. Mr. Speaker, Mr. President, distinguished Members of Congress, honored guests, and fellow citizens. May I congratulate all of you who are Members of this historic 100th Congress of the United States of America. In this 200th anniversary year of our Constitution, you and I stand on the shoulders of giants—men whose words and deeds put wind in the sails of freedom.

However, we must always remember that our Constitution is to be celebrated not for being old, but for being young—young with the same energy, spirit, and promise that filled each eventful day in Philadelphia's statehouse. We will be guided tonight by their acts, and we will be guided forever by their words....

Let's roll up our sleeves and go to work and put America's economic engine at full throttle. We can also be heartened by our progress across the world. Most important, America is at peace tonight, and freedom is on the march. And we've done much these past years to restore our defenses, our alliances, and our leadership in the world. Our sons and daughters in the services once again wear their uniforms with pride.

But though we've made much progress, I have one major regret: I took a risk with regard to our action in Iran. It did not work, and for that I assume full responsibility. The goals were worthy. I do not believe it was wrong to try to establish contacts with a country of strategic importance or to try to save lives. And certainly it was not wrong to try to secure freedom for our citizens held in barbaric captivity. But we did not achieve what we wished, and serious mistakes were made in trying to do so. We will get to the bottom of this, and I will take whatever action is called for.

But in debating the past ... we must not deny ourselves the successes of the future. Let it never be said of this generation of Americans that we became so obsessed with failure that we refused to take risks that could further the cause of peace and freedom in the world. Much is at stake here, and the Nation and the world are watching—to see if we go forward together in the national interest or if we let partisanship weaken us.

And let there be no mistake about American policy—we will not sit idly by if our interests or our friends in the Middle East are threatened, nor will we yield to terrorist blackmail. And now, ladies and gentlemen of the Congress, why don't we get to work?

I am pleased to report that because of our efforts to rebuild the strength of America, the world is a safer place. Earlier this month I submitted a budget to defend America and maintain our momentum to make up for neglect in the last decade. Well, I ask you to vote out a defense and foreign affairs budget that says "yes" to protecting our country. While the world is safer, it is not safe....

The Soviet Union says it wants a peaceful settlement in Afghanistan, yet it continues a brutal war and props up a regime whose days are clearly numbered. We are ready to support a political solution that guarantees the rapid withdrawal of all Soviet troops and genuine self-determination for the Afghan people.

.... Our commitment to a Western Hemisphere safe from aggression did not occur by spontaneous generation on the day that we took office. It began with the Monroe Doctrine in 1823 and continues our historic bipartisan American policy. Franklin Roosevelt said we "are determined to do everything possible to maintain peace on this hemisphere." President Truman was very blunt:

> "International communism seeks to crush and undermine and destroy the independence of the Americas. We cannot let that happen here."

And John F. Kennedy made clear that "Communist domination in this hemisphere can never be negotiated." Some in this Congress may choose to depart from this historic commitment, but I will not.

.... This 100th Congress has high responsibilities. I begin with a gentle reminder that many of these are simply the incomplete obligations of the past. The American people deserve to be impatient, because we do not yet have the public house in order. We've had great success in restoring our economic integrity, and we've rescued our nation from the worst economic mess since the

Depression. But there's more to do. For starters, the Federal deficit is outrageous. For years I've asked that we stop pushing onto our children the excesses of our government. And what the Congress finally needs to do is pass a constitutional amendment that mandates a balanced budget and forces government to live within its means. States, cities, and the families of America balance their budgets. Why can't we?

.... It's widely said that America is losing her competitive edge. Well, that won't happen if we act now. How well prepared are we to enter the 21st century? In my lifetime, America set the standard for the world. It is now time to determine that we should enter the next century having achieved a level of excellence unsurpassed in history. We will achieve this, first, by guaranteeing that government does everything possible to promote America's ability to compete. Second, we must act as individuals in a quest for excellence that will not be measured by new proposals or billions in new funding. Rather, it involves an expenditure of American spirit and just plain American grit....

Preparing for the future must begin, as always, with our children. We need to set for them new and more rigorous goals. We must demand more of ourselves and our children by raising literacy levels dramatically by the year 2000. Our children should master the basic concepts of math and science, and let's insist that students not leave high school until they have studied and understood the basic documents of our national heritage....

The responsibility of freedom presses us towards higher knowledge and, I believe, moral and spiritual greatness. Through lower taxes and smaller government, government has its ways of freeing people's spirits. But only we, each of us, can let the spirit soar against our own individual standards. Excellence is what makes freedom ring. And isn't that what we do best?

We're entering our third century now, but it's wrong to judge our nation by its years. The calendar can't measure America because we were meant to be an endless experiment in freedom—with no limit to our reaches, no boundaries to what we can do, no end point to our hopes.

The United States Constitution is the impassioned and inspired vehicle by which we travel through history. It grew out of the most fundamental inspiration of our existence: that we are here to serve Him by living free—that living free releases in us the noblest of impulses and the best of our abilities; that we would use these gifts for good and generous purposes and would secure them not just for ourselves and for our children but for all mankind.

Over the years—I won't count if you don't—nothing has been so heartwarming to me as speaking to America's young, and the little ones especially—so fresh-faced and so eager to know—well, from time to time I've been with them—they will ask about our Constitution. And I hope you Members of Congress will not deem this a breach of protocol if you'll permit me to share these thoughts again with the young people who might be listening or watching this evening.

I have read the constitutions of a number of countries, including the Soviet Union's. Now, some people are surprised to hear that they have a constitution, and it even supposedly grants a number of freedoms to its people. Many countries have written into their constitution provisions for freedom of speech and freedom of assembly. Well, if this is true, why is the Constitution of the United States so exceptional?

Well, the difference is so small that it almost escapes you—but it's so great it tells you the whole story in just three words: We the people. In those other constitutions, the Government tells the people of those countries what they're allowed to do. In our Constitution, we the people tell the Government what it can do, and it can do only those things listed in that document and no others.

Virtually every other revolution in history has just exchanged one set of rulers for another set of rulers. Our revolution is the first to say the people are the masters and government is their servant.

And you young people out there, don't ever forget that. Someday you could be in this room—but wherever you are, America is depending on you to reach your highest and be your best because here in America, we the people are in charge.

Just three words: We the people. Those are the kids on Christmas Day looking out from a frozen sentry post on the 38th parallel in Korea or aboard an aircraft carrier in the Mediterranean. A million miles from home, but doing their duty.

We the people. Those are the warm-hearted whose numbers we can't begin to count, who'll begin the day with a little prayer for hostages they will never know and MIA families they will never meet. Why? Because that's the way we are, this unique breed we call Americans.

We the people. They're farmers on tough times, but who never stop feeding a hungry world. They're the volunteers at the hospital choking back their tears for the hundredth time, caring for a baby struggling for life because of a mother who used drugs. And you'll forgive me a special memory—it's a million mothers like Nelle Reagan who never knew a stranger or turned a hungry person away from her kitchen door.

We the people. They refute last week's television commentary downgrading our optimism and our idealism. They are the entrepreneurs, the builders, the pioneers, and a lot of regular folks—the true heroes of our land who make up the most uncommon nation of doers in history. You know they're Americans because their spirit is as big as the universe and their hearts are bigger than their spirits.

We the people. Starting the third century of a dream and standing up to some cynic who's trying to tell us we're not going to get any better.

Are we at the end? Well, I can't tell it any better than the real thing—a story recorded by James Madison from the final moments of the Constitutional Convention—September 17th, 1787. As the last few members signed the document, Benjamin Franklin—the oldest delegate at eighty-one years and in frail health—looked over toward the chair where George Washington daily presided. At the back of the chair was painted the picture of a sun on the horizon. And turning to those sitting next to him, Franklin observed that artists found it difficult in their painting to distinguish between a rising and a setting sun.

Well, I know if we were there, we could see those delegates sitting around Franklin—leaning in to listen more closely to him. And then Dr. Franklin began to share his deepest hopes and fears about the outcome of their efforts, and this is what he said: "I have often looked at that picture behind the President without being able to tell whether it was a rising or setting sun: But now at length I have the happiness to know that it is a rising and not a setting sun."

Well, you can bet it's rising because, my fellow citizens, America isn't finished—her best days have just begun.

Thank you, God bless you and God bless America.

The Iran-Contra Controversy
March 4, 1987

President Reagan, upon learning that without his knowledge the Government had, in defiance of Congressional restrictions, secretly sold weapons to Iran and used the proceeds to fund Nicaragua's Contra rebels, took full responsibility for the actions of his subordinates.

My fellow Americans: I've spoken to you from this historic office on many occasions and about many things. The power of the Presidency is often thought to reside within this Oval Office. Yet it doesn't rest here; it rests in you, the American people, and in your trust. Your trust is what gives a President his powers of leadership and his personal strength, and it's what I want to talk to you about this evening.

For the past three months, I've been silent on the revelations about Iran. And you must have been thinking: "Well, why doesn't he tell us what's happening? Why doesn't he just speak to us as he has in the past when we've faced troubles or tragedies?" Others of you, I guess, were thinking: "What's he doing hiding out in the White House?" Well, the reason I haven't spoken to you before now is this: You deserve the truth. And as frustrating as the waiting has been, I felt it was improper to come to you with sketchy reports, or possibly even erroneous statements, which would then have to be corrected, creating even more doubt and confusion. There's been enough of that.

I've paid a price for my silence in terms of your trust and confidence. But I've had to wait, as you have, for the complete story. That's why I appointed [a] … special counselor to help get out the thousands of documents to the various investigations. And I appointed a special review Board, the Tower board, which took on the chore of pulling the truth together for me and getting to the bottom of things. It has now issued its findings.

I'm often accused of being an optimist, and it's true I had to hunt pretty hard to find any good news in the Board's report. As you know, it's well-stocked with criticisms, which I'll discuss in a moment; but I was very relieved to read this sentence: "… the Board is convinced that the President does indeed want the full story to be told." And that will continue to be my pledge to you as the other investigations go forward....

I've studied the Board's report. Its findings are honest, convincing, and highly critical; and I accept them. And tonight I want to share with you my thoughts on these findings and report to you on the actions I'm taking to implement the Board's recommendations.

First, let me say I take full responsibility for my own actions and for those of my administration. As angry as I may be about activities undertaken without my knowledge, I am still accountable for those activities. As disappointed as I may be in some who served me, I'm still the one who must answer to the American people for this behavior. And as personally distasteful as I find secret bank accounts and diverted funds—well, as the Navy would say, this happened on my watch.

Let's start with the part that is the most controversial. A few months ago I told the American people I did not trade arms for hostages. My heart and my best intentions still tell me that's true, but the facts and the evidence tell me it is not. As the Tower board reported, what began as a strategic opening to Iran deteriorated, in its implementation, into trading arms for hostages. This runs counter to my own beliefs, to administration policy, and to the original strategy we had in mind. There are reasons why it happened, but no excuses. It was a mistake.

I undertook the original Iran initiative in order to develop relations with those who might assume leadership in a post-Khomeini government. It's clear from the Board's report, however, that I let my personal concern for the hostages spill over into the geopolitical strategy of reaching out to Iran. I asked so many questions about the hostages welfare that I didn't ask enough about the specifics of the total Iran plan.

Let me say to the hostage families: We have not given up. We never will. And I promise you we'll use every legitimate means to free your loved ones from captivity. But I must also caution that those Americans who freely remain in such dangerous areas must know that they're responsible for their own safety.

Now, another major aspect of the Board's findings regards the transfer of funds to the Nicaraguan Contras. The Tower Board wasn't able to find out what happened to this money, so the facts here will be left to the continuing investigations of the court-appointed Independent Counsel and the two congressional investigating committees. I'm confident the truth will come out about this matter, as well. As I told the Tower board, I didn't know about any diversion of funds to the contras. But as President, I cannot escape responsibility.

Much has been said about my management style, a style that's worked successfully for me during 8 years as Governor of California and for most of my Presidency. The way I work is to identify the problem, find the right individuals to do the job, and then let them go to it. I've found this invariably brings out the best in people. They seem to rise to their full capability, and in the long run you get more done.

When it came to managing the NSC staff, let's face it, my style didn't match its previous track record. I've already begun correcting this. As a start, yesterday I met with the entire professional staff of the National Security Council. I defined for them the values I want to guide the national security policies of this country. I told them that I wanted a policy that was as justifiable and understandable in public as it was in secret. I wanted a policy that reflected the will of the Congress as well as of the White House. And I told them that there'll be no more freelancing by individuals when it comes to our national security.

You've heard a lot about the staff of the National Security Council in recent months. Well, I can tell you, they are good and dedicated government employees, who put in long hours for the Nation's benefit. They are eager and anxious to serve their country.

One thing still upsetting me, however, is that no one kept proper records of meetings or decisions. This led to my failure to recollect whether I approved an arms shipment before or after the fact. I did approve it; I just can't say specifically when. Well, rest assured, there's plenty of recordkeeping now going on at 1600 Pennsylvania Avenue.

For nearly a week now, I've been studying the Board's report. I want the American people to know that this wrenching ordeal of recent months has not been in vain. I endorse every one of the Tower Board's recommendations. In fact, I'm going beyond its recommendations so as to put the house in even better order.

I'm taking action in three basic areas: personnel, national security policy, and the process for making sure that the system works. First, personnel—I've brought in an accomplished and highly respected new team here at the White House. They bring new blood, new energy, and new credibility and experience....

Second, in the area of national security policy, I have ordered the NSC to begin a comprehensive review of all covert operations. I have also directed that any covert activity be in support of clear policy objectives and in compliance with American values. I expect a covert policy that, if Americans saw it on the front page of their newspaper, they'd say, "That makes sense." I have had issued a directive prohibiting the NSC staff itself from undertaking covert operations—no ifs, ands, or buts. I have asked Vice President Bush to reconvene his task force on terrorism to review our terrorist policy in light of the events that have occurred.

Third, in terms of the process of reaching national security decisions, I am adopting in total the Tower Report's model of how the NSC process and staff should work. I am directing [Frank] Carlucci to take the necessary steps to make that happen. He will report back to me on further reforms that might be needed. I've created the post of NSC legal adviser to assure a greater sensitivity to matters of law.

I am also determined to make the congressional oversight process work. Proper procedures for consultation with the Congress will be followed, not only in letter but in spirit. Before the end of March, I will report to the Congress on all the steps I've taken in line with the Tower Board's conclusions.

Now, what should happen when you make a mistake is this: You take your knocks, you learn your lessons, and then you move on. That's the healthiest way to deal with a problem. This in no way diminishes the importance of the other continuing investigations, but the business of our country and our people must proceed. I've gotten this message from Republicans and Democrats in Congress, from allies around the world, and—if we're reading the signals right—even from the Soviets. And of course, I've heard the message from you, the American people. You know, by the time you reach my age, you've made plenty of mistakes. And if you've lived your life properly—so, you learn. You put things in perspective. You pull your energies together. You change. You go forward.

My fellow Americans, I have a great deal that I want to accomplish with you and for you over the next two years. And the Lord willing, that's exactly what I intend to do.

Good night, and God bless you.

Tear Down This Wall!
June 12, 1987

At West Berlin's Brandenberg Gate, President Reagan demanded the destruction of the most infamous symbol of the Cold War.

Twenty-four years ago, President John F. Kennedy visited Berlin, speaking to the people of this city and the world at the city hall. Well, since then two other presidents have come, each in his turn, to Berlin. And today I, myself, make my second visit to your city.

We come to Berlin, we American Presidents, because it's our duty to speak, in this place, of freedom. But I must confess, we're drawn here by other things as well: by the feeling of history in this city, more than 500 years older than our own nation; by the beauty of the Grunewald and the Tiergarten; most of all, by your courage and determination. Perhaps the composer, Paul Lincke, understood something about American Presidents. You see, like so many Presidents before me, I come here today because wherever I go, whatever I do: "Ich hab noch einen koffer in Berlin." [I still have a suitcase in Berlin.]

Our gathering today is being broadcast throughout Western Europe and North America. I understand that it is being seen and heard as well in the East.... To those listening in East Berlin, a special word: Although I cannot be with you, I address my remarks to you just as surely as to those standing here before me. For I join you, as I join your fellow countrymen in the West, in this firm, this unalterable belief: Es gibt nur ein Berlin. [There is only one Berlin.]

Behind me stands a wall that encircles the free sectors of this city, part of a vast system of barriers that divides the entire continent of Europe. From the Baltic, south, those barriers cut across Germany in a gash of barbed wire, concrete, dog runs, and guard towers. Farther south, there may be no visible, no obvious wall. But there remain armed guards and checkpoints all the same—still a restriction on the right to travel, still an instrument to impose upon ordinary men and women the will of a totalitarian state. Yet it is here in Berlin where the wall emerges most clearly; here, cutting across your city, where the news photo and the television screen have imprinted this brutal division of a continent upon the mind of the world. Standing before the Brandenburg Gate, every man is a German, separated from his fellow men. Every man is a Berliner, forced to look upon a scar. President von Weizsacker has said: "The German question is open as long as the Brandenburg Gate is closed." Today I say: As long as this gate is closed, as long as this scar of a wall is permitted to stand, it is not the German question alone that remains open, but the question of freedom for all mankind. Yet I do not come here to lament. For I find in Berlin a message of hope—even in the shadow of this wall, a message of triumph.

In this season of spring in 1945, the people of Berlin emerged from their air raid shelters to find devastation. Thousands of miles away, the people of the United States reached out to help. And in 1947 Secretary of State—as you've been told—George Marshall announced the creation of what would become known as the Marshall plan. Speaking precisely forty years ago this month, he said: "Our policy is directed not against any country or doctrine, but against hunger, poverty, desperation, and chaos."

In the Reichstag a few moments ago, I saw a display commemorating this 40th anniversary of the Marshall plan. I was struck by the sign on a burnt-out, gutted structure that was being rebuilt. I understand that Berliners of my own generation can remember seeing signs like it dotted throughout the Western sectors of the city. The sign read simply: "The Marshall plan is helping here to strengthen the free world." A strong, free world in the West, that dream became real. Japan rose from ruin to become an economic giant. Italy, France, Belgium—virtually every nation in Western Europe saw political and economic rebirth; the European Community was founded....

Where four decades ago there was rubble, today in West Berlin there is the greatest industrial output of any city in Germany—busy office blocks, fine homes and apartments, proud avenues, and the spreading lawns of park land. Where a city's culture seemed to have been destroyed, today there are two great universities, orchestras and an opera, countless theaters, and museums. Where there was want, today there's abundance—food, clothing, automobiles—the wonderful goods of the Ku'damm. From devastation, from utter ruin, you Berliners have, in freedom, rebuilt a city that once again ranks as one of the greatest on Earth. The Soviets may have had other plans. But, my friends, there were a few things the Soviets didn't count on Berliner herz, Berliner humor, ja, und Berliner schnauze. [Berliner heart, Berliner humor, yes, and a Berliner schnauze.]

In the 1950's, Khrushchev predicted: "We will bury you." But in the West today, we see a free world that has achieved a level of prosperity and well-being unprecedented in all human history. In the Communist world, we see failure, technological backwardness, declining standards of health, even want of the most basic kind—too little food. Even today, the Soviet Union still cannot feed itself. After these four decades, then, there stands before the entire world one great and inescapable conclusion: Freedom leads to prosperity. Freedom replaces the ancient hatreds among the nations with comity and peace. Freedom is the victor. And now the Soviets themselves may, in a limited way, be coming to understand the importance of freedom. We hear much from Moscow about a new policy of reform and openness. Some political prisoners have been released. Certain foreign news broadcasts are no longer being jammed. Some economic enterprises have been permitted to operate with greater freedom from state control. Are these the beginnings of profound changes in the Soviet state? Or are they token gestures, intended to raise false hopes in the West, or to strengthen the Soviet system without changing it? We welcome change and openness; for we believe that freedom and security go together, that the advance of human liberty can only strengthen the cause of world peace. There is one sign the Soviets can make that would be unmistakable, that would advance dramatically the cause of freedom and peace. General Secretary Gorbachev, if you seek peace, if you seek prosperity for the Soviet Union and Eastern Europe, if you seek liberalization: Come here to this gate! Mr. Gorbachev, open this gate! Mr. Gorbachev, tear down this wall!

Moscow State University Address
May 31, 1988

During his historic visit to the Soviet Union, President Reagan was invited to speak directly to the students of the prestigious Moscow State University.

Before I left Washington, I received many heartfelt letters and telegrams asking me to carry here a simple message—perhaps, but also some of the most important business of this summit—it is a message of peace and good will and hope for a growing friendship and closeness between our two peoples.

First I want to take a little time to talk to you much as I would to any group of university students in the United States. I want to talk not just of the realities of today but of the possibilities of tomorrow.

You know, one of the first contacts between your country and mine took place between Russian and American explorers. The Americans were members of Cook's last voyage on an expedition searching for an Arctic passage; on the island of Unalaska, they came upon the Russians, who took them in, and together with the native inhabitants, held a prayer service on the ice.

The explorers of the modern era are the entrepreneurs, men with vision, with the courage to take risks and faith enough to brave the unknown. These entrepreneurs and their small enterprises are responsible for almost all the economic growth in the United States. They are the prime movers of the technological revolution. In fact, one of the largest personal computer firms in the United States was started by two college students, no older than you, in the garage behind their home.

Some people, even in my own country, look at the riot of experiment that is the free market and see only waste. What of all the entrepreneurs that fail? Well, many do, particularly the successful ones; often several times. And if you ask them the secret of their success, they'll tell you it's all that they learned in their struggles along the way—yes, it's what they learned from failing. Like an athlete in competition or a scholar in pursuit of the truth, experience is the greatest teacher.

We are seeing the power of economic freedom spreading around the world—places such as the Republic of Korea, Singapore, Taiwan have vaulted into the technological era, barely pausing in the industrial age along the way. Low-tax agricultural policies in the subcontinent mean that in some years India is now a net exporter of food. Perhaps most exciting are the winds of change that are blowing over the People's Republic of China, where one-quarter of the world's population is now getting its first taste of economic freedom.

At the same time, the growth of democracy has become one of the most powerful political movements of our age. In Latin America in the 1970's, only a third of the population lived under democratic government; today over 90 percent does. In the Philippines, in the Republic of Korea, free, contested, democratic elections are the order of the day. Throughout the world, free markets are the model for growth. Democracy is the standard by which governments are measured.

We Americans make no secret of our belief in freedom. In fact, it's something of a national pastime. Every 4 years the American people choose a new President, and 1988 is one of those years. At one point there were 13 major candidates running in the two major parties, not to mention all the others, including the Socialist and Libertarian candidates—all trying to get my job.

About 1,000 local television stations, 8,500 radio stations, and 1,700 daily newspapers, each one an independent, private enterprise, fiercely independent of the Government, report on the candidates, grill them in interviews, and bring them together for debates. In the end, the people vote—they decide who will be the next President.

But freedom doesn't begin or end with elections. Go to any American town, to take just an example, and you'll see dozens of synagogues and mosques—and you'll see families of every conceivable nationality worshiping together.

Go into any schoolroom, and there you will see children being taught the Declaration of Independence, that they are endowed by their Creator with certain unalienable rights—among them life, liberty, and the pursuit of happiness—that no government can justly deny—the guarantees in their Constitution for freedom of speech, freedom of assembly, and freedom of religion.

Go into any courtroom, and there will preside an independent judge, beholden to no government power. There every defendant has the right to a trial by a jury of his peers, usually twelve men and women—common citizens—they are the ones, the only ones, who weigh the evidence and decide on guilt or innocence. In that court, the accused is innocent until proven guilty, and the word of a policeman or any official has no greater legal standing than the word of the accused.

Go to any university campus, and there you'll find an open, sometimes heated discussion of the problems in American society and what can be done to correct them. Turn on the television, and you'll see the legislature conducting the business of government right there before the camera, debating and voting on the legislation that will become the law of the land. March in any demonstration, and there are many of them—the people's right of assembly is guaranteed in the Constitution and protected by the police.

But freedom is more even than this. Freedom is the right to question and change the established way of doing things. It is the continuing revolution of the marketplace. It is the understanding that allows us to recognize shortcomings and seek solutions. It is the right to put forth an idea, scoffed at by the experts, and watch it catch fire among the people. It is the right to stick—to dream—to follow your dream, or stick to your conscience, even if you're the only one in a sea of doubters.

Freedom is the recognition that no single person, no single authority or government has a monopoly on the truth, but that every individual life is infinitely precious, that every one of us put on this world has been put there for a reason and has something to offer.

America is a nation made up of hundreds of nationalities. Our ties to you are more than ones of good feeling; they're ties of kinship. In America, you'll find Russians, Armenians, Ukrainians, peoples from Eastern Europe and Central Asia. They come from every part of this vast continent, from every continent, to live in harmony, seeking a place where each cultural heritage is respected, each is valued for its diverse strengths and beauties and the richness it brings to our lives.

Recently, a few individuals and families have been allowed to visit relatives in the West. We can only hope that it won't be long before all are allowed to do so and Ukrainian-Americans, Baltic-Americans, Armenian-Americans can freely visit their homelands, just as this Irish-American visits his.

Freedom, it has been said, makes people selfish and materialistic, but Americans are one of the most religious peoples on Earth. Because they know that liberty, just as life itself, is not earned but a gift from God, they seek to share that gift with the world. "Reason and experience," said George Washington in his farewell address, "both forbid us to expect that national morality can prevail in exclusion of religious principle. And it is substantially true, that virtue or morality is a necessary spring of popular government."

Democracy is less a system of government than it is a system to keep government limited, unintrusive. A system of constraints on power to keep politics and government secondary to the important things in life, the true sources of value found only in family and faith.

I have often said, nations do not distrust each other because they are armed; they are armed because they distrust each other. If this globe is to live in peace and prosper, if it is to embrace all the possibilities of the technological revolution, then nations must renounce, once and for all, the right to an expansionist foreign policy. Peace between nations must be an enduring goal—not a tactical stage in a continuing conflict.

I've been told that there's a popular song in your country—perhaps you know it—whose evocative refrain asks the question, "Do the Russians want a war?" In answer it says, "Go ask that silence lingering in the air, above the birch and poplar there, beneath those trees the soldiers lie. Go ask my mother, ask my wife; then you will have to ask no more, `Do the Russians want a war?'"

But what of your one-time allies? What of those who embraced you on the Elbe? What if we were to ask the watery graves of the Pacific or the European battlefields where America's fallen were buried far from home? What if we were to ask their mothers, sisters, and sons, do Americans want war? Ask us, too, and you'll find the same answer, the same longing in every heart. People do not make wars; governments do—and no mother would ever willingly sacrifice her sons for territorial gain, for economic advantage, for ideology. A people free to choose will always choose peace.

Americans seek always to make friends of old antagonists. After a colonial revolution with Britain, we have cemented for all ages the ties of kinship between our nations. After a terrible Civil War between North and South, we healed our wounds and found true unity as a nation. We fought two world wars in my lifetime against Germany and one with Japan, but now the Federal Republic of Germany and Japan are two of our closest allies and friends.

Some people point to the trade disputes between us as a sign of strain, but they're the frictions of all families, and the family of free nations is a big and vital and sometimes boisterous one. I can tell you that nothing would please my heart more than in my lifetime to see American and Soviet diplomats grappling with the problem of trade disputes between America and a growing, exuberant, exporting Soviet Union that had opened up to economic freedom and growth.

Is this just a dream? Perhaps, but it is a dream that is our responsibility to have come true.

Your generation is living in one of the most exciting, hopeful times in Soviet history. It is a time when the first breath of freedom stirs the air and the heart beats to the accelerated rhythm of hope, when the accumulated spiritual energies of a long silence yearn to break free.

We do not know what the conclusion will be of this journey, but we're hopeful that the promise of reform will be fulfilled. In this Moscow spring, this May 1988, we may be allowed that hope—that freedom, like the fresh green sapling planted over Tolstoy's grave, will blossom forth at last in the rich fertile soil of your people and culture. We may be allowed to hope that the marvelous sound of a new openness will keep rising through, ringing through, leading to a new world of reconciliation, friendship, and peace.

Thank you all very much, and *da blagoslovit vas gospod!* God bless you.

No Republicans, No Democrats, Just Americans
January 25, 1988

The President shall from time to time give to the Congress information on the State of the Union.

—The United States Constitution

When we first met here seven years ago—many of us for the first time—it was with the hope of beginning something new for America. We meet here tonight in this historic Chamber to continue that work. If anyone expects just a proud recitation of the accomplishments of my administration, I say let's leave that to history; we're not finished yet. So, my message to you tonight is put on your work shoes—we're still on the job.

History records the power of the ideas that brought us here those 7 years ago—ideas like the individual's right to reach as far and as high as his or her talents will permit; the free market as an engine of economic progress. And as an ancient Chinese philosopher, Lao-tzu, said, "Govern a great nation as you would cook a small fish; do not overdo it." Well, these ideas were part of a larger notion—a vision, if you will, of America herself—an America not only rich in opportunity for the individual but an America, too, of strong families and vibrant neighborhoods; an America whose divergent but harmonizing communities were a reflection of a deeper community of values—the value of work, of family, of religion, and of the love of freedom that God places in each of us and whose defense He has entrusted in a special way to this nation.

All of this was made possible by an idea I spoke of when Mr. Gorbachev was here—the belief that the most exciting revolution ever known to humankind began with three simple words: "We the People"—the revolutionary notion that the people grant government its rights, and not the other way around. And there's one lesson that has come home powerfully to me, which I would offer to you now. Just as those who created this Republic pledged to each other their lives, their fortunes, and their sacred honor, so, too, America's leaders today must pledge to each other that we will keep foremost in our hearts and minds not what is best for ourselves or for our party but what is best for America. In the spirit of Jefferson, let us affirm that in this Chamber tonight there are no Republicans, no Democrats, just Americans.

Yes, we will have our differences, but let us always remember—what unites us far outweighs whatever divides us. Those who sent us here to serve them—the millions of Americans watching and listening tonight—expect this of us. Let's prove to them and to ourselves that democracy works even in an election year.... Tonight, then, we're strong, prosperous, at peace, and we are free. This is the state of our Union. And if we will work together this year, I believe we can give a future President and a future Congress the chance to make that prosperity, that peace, that freedom not just the state of our Union but the state of our world.... My friends, some years ago, the Federal Government declared war on poverty, and poverty won. Today the Federal Government has fifty-nine major welfare programs and spends more than $100 billion a year on them. What has all this money done? Well, too often it has only made poverty harder to escape. Federal welfare programs have created a massive social problem. With the best of intentions, government created a poverty trap that wreaks havoc on the very support system the poor need most to lift themselves out of poverty—the family. Dependency has become the one enduring heirloom, passed from one generation to the next, of too many fragmented families. It is time—this may be the most radical thing I've said in seven years in this office—it's time for Washington to show a little humility. There are a thousand sparks of genius in fifty States and a thousand communities around the Nation. It is time to nurture them and see which ones can catch fire and become guiding lights.

States have begun to show us the way. They've demonstrated that successful welfare programs can be built around more effective child support enforcement practices and innovative programs requiring welfare recipients to work or prepare for work. Let us give the States more flexibility and encourage more reforms. Let's start making our welfare system the first rung on America's ladder of opportunity—a boost up from dependency, not a graveyard but a birthplace of hope.

And now let me turn to three other matters vital to family values and the quality of family life. The first is an untold American success story. Recently, we released our annual survey of what graduating high school seniors have to say about drugs. Cocaine use is declining, and marijuana use was the lowest since surveying began. We can be proud that our students are "just saying no" to drugs. But let us remember what this menace requires—commitment from every part of America and every single American—a commitment to a drug-free America. The war against drugs is a war of individual battles, a crusade with many heroes—including America's young people and also someone very special to me. She has helped so many of our young people to say "no" to drugs. Nancy, much credit belongs to you, and I want to express to you your husband's pride and your country's thanks. Surprised you, didn't I?

.... We've seen such changes in the world in seven years—as totalitarianism struggles to avoid being overwhelmed by the forces of economic advance and the aspiration for human freedom, it is the free nations that are resilient and resurgent. As the global democratic revolution has put totalitarianism on the defensive, we have left behind the days of retreat—America is again a vigorous leader of the free world, a nation that acts decisively and firmly in the furtherance of her principles and vital interests. No legacy would make me more proud than leaving in place a bipartisan consensus for the cause of world freedom, a consensus that prevents a paralysis of American power from ever occurring again. But my thoughts tonight go beyond this, and I hope you'll let me end this evening with a personal reflection. You know, the world could never be quite the same again after Jacob Shallus, a trustworthy and dependable clerk of the Pennsylvania General Assembly, took his pen and engrossed those words about representative government in the preamble of our Constitution. And in a quiet but final way, the course of human events was forever altered when, on a ridge overlooking the Emmitsburg Pike in an obscure Pennsylvania town called Gettysburg, Lincoln spoke of our duty to government of and by the people and never letting it perish from the Earth.

At the start of this decade, I suggested that we live in equally momentous times—that it is up to us now to decide whether our form of government would endure and whether history still had a place of greatness for a quiet, pleasant, greening land called America. Not everything has been made perfect in seven years—nor will it be made perfect in seven times seventy years—but before us, this year and beyond, are great prospects for the cause of peace and world freedom. It means, too, that the young Americans I spoke of seven years ago, as well as those who might be coming along the Virginia or

Maryland shores this night and seeing for the first time the lights of this capital city, the lights that cast their glow on our great halls of government and the monuments to the memory of our great men—it means those young Americans will find a city of hope in a land that is free. We can be proud that for them and for us, as those lights along the Potomac are still seen this night—signaling as they have for nearly two centuries and as we pray God they always will, that another generation of Americans has protected and passed on lovingly this place called America, this shining city on a hill, this government of, by, and for the people. Thank you, and God bless you.

Farewell Address
January 11, 1989

Having served two terms as President of the United States, Ronald Reagan gave a heartfelt farewell address to the nation.

This is the thirty-fourth time I'll speak to you from the Oval Office and the last. We've been together eight years now, and soon it'll be time for me to go. But before I do, I wanted to share some thoughts, some of which I've been saving for a long time. It's been the honor of my life to be your President. So many of you have written the past few weeks to say thanks, but I could say as much to you. Nancy and I are grateful for the opportunity you gave us to serve.

One of the things about the Presidency is that you're always somewhat apart. You spend a lot of time going by too fast in a car someone else is driving, and seeing the people through tinted glass—the parents holding up a child, and the wave you saw too late and couldn't return. And so many times I wanted to stop and reach out from behind the glass, and connect. Well, maybe I can do a little of that tonight. People ask how I feel about leaving. And the fact is, "parting is such sweet sorrow." The sweet part is California and the ranch and freedom. The sorrow—the goodbyes, of course, and leaving this beautiful place.

You know, down the hall and up the stairs from this office is the part of the White House where the President and his family live. There are a few favorite windows I have up there that I like to stand and look out of early in the morning. The view is over the grounds here to the Washington Monument, and then the Mall and the Jefferson Memorial. But on mornings when the humidity is low, you can see past the Jefferson to the river, the Potomac, and the Virginia shore. Someone said that's the view Lincoln had when he saw the smoke rising from the Battle of Bull Run. I see more prosaic things: the grass on the banks, the morning traffic as people make their way to work, now and then a sailboat on the river.

I've been thinking a bit at that window. I've been reflecting on what the past eight years have meant and mean. And the image that comes to mind like a refrain is a nautical one—a small story about a big ship, and a refugee, and a sailor. It was back in the early '80s, at the height of the boat people. And the sailor was hard at work on the carrier Midway, which was patrolling the South China Sea. The sailor, like most American servicemen, was young, smart, and fiercely observant. The crew spied on the horizon a leaky little boat. And crammed inside were refugees from Indochina hoping to get to America. The Midway sent a small launch to bring them to the ship and safety. As the refugees made their way through the choppy seas, one spied the sailor on deck, and stood up, and called out to him. He yelled, "Hello, American sailor. Hello, freedom man."

A small moment with a big meaning, a moment the sailor, who wrote it in a letter, couldn't get out of his mind. And, when I saw it, neither could I. Because that's what it was to be an American in the 1980's. We stood, again, for freedom. I know we always have, but in the past few years the world again—and in a way, we ourselves—rediscovered it. It's been quite a journey this decade, and we held together through some stormy seas. And at the end, together, we are reaching our destination.

The fact is, from Grenada to the Washington and Moscow summits, from the recession of '81 to '82, to the expansion that began in late '82 and continues to this day, we've made a difference. The way I see it, there were two great triumphs, two things that I'm proudest of. One is the economic recovery, in which the people of America created—and filled—nineteen million new jobs. The other is the recovery of our morale. America is respected again in the world and looked to for leadership.

Something that happened to me a few years ago reflects some of this. It was back in 1981, and I was attending my first big economic summit, which was held that year in Canada. The meeting place rotates among the member countries. The opening meeting was a formal dinner for the heads of government of the seven industrialized nations. Now, I sat there like the new kid in school and listened, and it was all Francois this and Helmut that. They dropped titles and spoke to one another on a first-name basis. Well, at one point I sort of leaned in and said, "My name's Ron." Well, in that same year, we began the actions we felt would ignite an economic comeback—cut taxes and regulation, started to cut spending. And soon the recovery began. Two years later, another economic summit with pretty much the same cast. At the big opening meeting we all got together, and all of a sudden, just for a moment, I saw that everyone was just sitting there looking at me. And then one of them broke the silence. "Tell us about the American miracle," he said.

Well, back in 1980, when I was running for President, it was all so different. Some pundits said our programs would result in catastrophe. Our views on foreign affairs would cause war. Our plans for the economy would cause inflation to soar and bring about economic collapse. I even remember one highly respected economist saying, back in 1982, that "The engines of economic growth have shut down here, and they're likely to stay that way for years to come." Well, he and the other opinion leaders were wrong. The fact is, what they called "radical" was really "right." What they called "dangerous" was just "desperately needed."

And in all of that time I won a nickname, "The Great Communicator." But I never thought it was my style or the words I used that made a difference: it was the content. I wasn't a great communicator, but I communicated great things, and they didn't spring full bloom from my brow, they came from the heart of a great nation—from our experience, our wisdom, and our belief in the principles that have guided us for two centuries. They called it the Reagan revolution. Well, I'll accept that, but for me it always seemed more like the great rediscovery, a rediscovery of our values and our common sense.

Common sense told us that when you put a big tax on something, the people will produce less of it. So, we cut the people's tax rates, and the people produced more than ever before. The economy bloomed like a plant that had been cut back and could now grow quicker and stronger. Our economic program brought about the longest peacetime expansion in our history: real family income up, the poverty rate down, entrepreneurship booming, and an explosion in research and new technology. We're exporting more than ever because American industry became more competitive and at the same time, we summoned the national will to knock down protectionist walls abroad instead of erecting them at home.

Common sense also told us that to preserve the peace, we'd have to become strong again after years of weakness and confusion. So, we rebuilt our defenses, and this New Year we toasted the new peacefulness around the globe. Not only have the superpowers actually begun to reduce their stockpiles of nuclear weapons—and hope for even more progress is bright—but the regional conflicts that rack the globe are also beginning to cease. The Persian Gulf is no longer a war zone. The Soviets are leaving Afghanistan. The Vietnamese are preparing to pull out of Cambodia, and an American-mediated accord will soon send 50,000 Cuban troops home from Angola.

The lesson of all this was, of course, that because we're a great nation, our challenges seem complex. It will always be this way. But as long as we remember our first principles and believe in ourselves, the future will always be ours. And something else we learned: Once you begin a great movement, there's no telling where it will end. We meant to change a nation, and instead, we changed a world. Countries across the globe are turning to free markets and free speech and turning away from the ideologies of the past. For them, the great rediscovery of the 1980's has been that, lo and behold, the moral way of government is the practical way of government: Democracy, the profoundly good, is also the profoundly productive.

When you've got to the point when you can celebrate the anniversaries of your thirty-ninth birthday you can sit back sometimes, review your life, and see it flowing before you. For me there was a fork in the river, and it was right in the middle of my life. I never meant to go into politics. It wasn't my intention when I was young. But I was raised to believe you had to pay your way for the blessings bestowed on you. I was happy with my career in the entertainment world, but I ultimately went into politics because I wanted to protect something precious.

Ours was the first revolution in the history of mankind that truly reversed the course of government, and with three little words: "We the People." "We the People" tell the government what to do; it doesn't tell us. "We the People" are the driver; the government is the car. And we decide where it should go, and by what route, and how fast. Almost all the world's constitutions are documents in which governments tell the people what their privileges are. Our Constitution is a document in which "We the People" tell the government what it is allowed to do. "We the People" are free. This belief has been the underlying basis for everything I've tried to do these past eight years.

But back in the 1960's, when I began, it seemed to me that we'd begun reversing the order of things—that through more and more rules and regulations and confiscatory taxes, the government was taking more of our money, more of our options, and more of our freedom. I went into politics in part to put up my hand and say, "Stop." I was a citizen politician, and it seemed the right thing for a citizen to do. I think we have stopped a lot of what needed stopping. And I hope we have once again reminded people that man is not free unless government is limited. There's a clear cause and effect here that is as neat and predictable as a law of physics: As government expands, liberty contracts.

Nothing is less free than pure Communism—and yet we have, the past few years, forged a satisfying new closeness with the Soviet Union. I've been asked if this isn't a gamble, and my answer is no because we're basing our actions not on words but deeds. The detente of the 1970's was based not on actions but promises. They'd promise to treat their own people and the people of the world better. But the gulag was still the gulag, and the state was still expansionist, and they still waged proxy wars in Africa, Asia, and Latin America. Well, this time, so far, it's different. President Gorbachev has brought about some internal democratic reforms and begun the withdrawal from Afghanistan. He has also freed prisoners whose names I've given him every time we've met.

But life has a way of reminding you of big things through small incidents. Once, during the heady days of the Moscow summit, Nancy and I decided to break off from the entourage one afternoon to visit the shops on Arbat Street—that's a little street just off Moscow's main shopping area. Even though our visit was a surprise, every Russian there immediately recognized us and called out our names and reached for our hands. We were just about swept away by the warmth. You could almost feel the possibilities in all that joy. But within seconds, a KGB detail pushed their way toward us and began pushing and shoving the people in the crowd. It was an interesting moment. It reminded me that while the man on the street in the Soviet Union yearns for peace, the government is Communist. And those who run it are Communists, and that means we and they view such issues as freedom and human rights very differently.

We must keep up our guard, but we must also continue to work together to lessen and eliminate tension and mistrust. My view is that

President Gorbachev is different from previous Soviet leaders. I think he knows some of the things wrong with his society and is trying to fix them. We wish him well. And we'll continue to work to make sure that the Soviet Union that eventually emerges from this process is a less threatening one. What it all boils down to is this: I want the new closeness to continue. And it will, as long as we make it clear that we will continue to act in a certain way as long as they continue to act in a helpful manner. If and when they don't, at first pull your punches. If they persist, pull the plug. It's still trust but verify. It's still play, but cut the cards. It's still watch closely. And don't be afraid to see what you see.

I've been asked if I have any regrets. Well, I do. The deficit is one. I've been talking a great deal about that lately, but tonight isn't for arguments, and I'm going to hold my tongue. But an observation: I've had my share of victories in the Congress, but what few people noticed is that I never won anything you didn't win for me. They never saw my troops, they never saw Reagan's regiments, the American people. You won every battle with every call you made and letter you wrote demanding action. Well, action is still needed. If we're to finish the job, Reagan's regiments will have to become the Bush brigades. Soon he'll be the chief, and he'll need you every bit as much as I did.

Finally, there is a great tradition of warnings in Presidential farewells, and I've got one that's been on my mind for some time. But oddly enough it starts with one of the things I'm proudest of in the past eight years: the resurgence of national pride that I called the new patriotism. This national feeling is good, but it won't count for much, and it won't last unless it's grounded in thoughtfulness and knowledge. An informed patriotism is what we want. And are we doing a good enough job teaching our children what America is and what she represents in the long history of the world? Those of us who are over thirty-five or so years of age grew up in a different America. We were taught, very directly, what it means to be an American. And we absorbed, almost in the air, a love of country and an appreciation of its institutions. If you didn't get these things from your family you got them from the neighborhood, from the father down the street who fought in Korea or the family who lost someone at Anzio. Or you could get a sense of patriotism from school. And if all else failed you could get a sense of patriotism from the popular culture. The movies celebrated democratic values and implicitly reinforced the idea that America was special. TV was like that, too, through the mid-'60s.

But now, we're about to enter the '90s, and some things have changed. Younger parents aren't sure that an unambivalent appreciation of America is the right thing to teach modern children. And as for those who create the popular culture, well-grounded patriotism is no longer the style. Our spirit is back, but we haven't reinstitutionalized it. We've got to do a better job of getting across that America is freedom—freedom of speech, freedom of religion, freedom of enterprise. And freedom is special and rare. It's fragile; it needs protection.

So, we've got to teach history based not on what's in fashion but what's important—why the Pilgrims came here, who Jimmy Doolittle was, and what those 30 seconds over Tokyo meant. You know, 4 years ago on the fortieth anniversary of D-Day, I read a letter from a young woman writing to her late father, who'd fought on Omaha Beach. Her name was Lisa Zanatta Henn, and she said, "we will always remember, we will never forget what the boys of Normandy did." Well, let's help her keep her word. If we forget what we did, we won't know who we are. I'm warning of an eradication of the American memory that could result, ultimately, in an erosion of the American spirit. Let's start with some basics: more attention to American history and a greater emphasis on civic ritual.

And let me offer lesson number one about America: All great change in America begins at the dinner table. So, tomorrow night in the kitchen I hope the talking begins. And children, if your parents haven't been teaching you what it means to be an American, let 'em know and nail 'em on it. That would be a very American thing to do. And that's about all I have to say tonight, except for one thing. The past few days when I've been at that window upstairs, I've thought a bit of the "shining city upon a hill." The phrase comes from John Winthrop, who wrote it to describe the America he imagined. What he imagined was important because he was an early Pilgrim, an early freedom man. He journeyed here on what today we'd call a little wooden boat; and like the other Pilgrims, he was looking for a home that would be free. I've spoken of the shining city all my political life, but I don't know if I ever quite communicated what I saw when I said it. But in my mind it was a tall, proud city built on rocks stronger than oceans, wind-swept, God-blessed, and teeming with people of all kinds living in harmony and peace; a city with free ports that hummed with commerce and creativity. And if there had to be city walls, the walls had doors and the doors were open to anyone with the will and the heart to get here. That's how I saw it, and see it still.

And how stands the city on this winter night? More prosperous, more secure, and happier than it was eight years ago. But more than that: After two hundred years, two centuries, she still stands strong and true on the granite ridge, and her glow has held steady no matter what storm. And she's still a beacon, still a magnet for all who must have freedom, for all the pilgrims from all the lost places who are hurtling through the darkness, toward home.

We've done our part. And as I walk off into the city streets, a final word to the men and women of the Reagan revolution, the men and women across America who for eight years did the work that brought America back. My friends: We did it. We weren't just marking time. We made a difference. We made the city stronger, we made the city freer, and we left her in good hands. All in all, not bad, not bad at all. And so, goodbye, God bless you, and God bless the United States of America.

An Empire Of Ideals
August 17, 1992

Ronald Reagan said his farewell to the Republican Party at their National Convention in Houston, Texas.

Over the years, I've addressed this convention as a private citizen, as a governor, as a presidential candidate, as a president and now, once again tonight, as private citizen Ronald Reagan.

…. I have not only seen, but lived the marvels of what historians have called the "American Century." Yet, tonight is not a time to look backward. For while I take inspiration from the past, like most Americans, I live for the future. So this evening, for just a few minutes, I hope you will let me talk about a country that is forever young.

There was a time when empires were defined by land mass, subjugated peoples, and military might. But the United States is unique because we are an empire of ideals. For two hundred years we have been set apart by our faith in the ideals of democracy, of free men and free markets, and of the extraordinary possibilities that lie within seemingly ordinary men and women. We believe that no power of government is as formidable a force for good as the creativity and entrepreneurial drive of the American people.

Those are the ideals that invented revolutionary technologies and a culture envied by people everywhere. This powerful sense of energy has made America synonymous for opportunity the world over. And after generations of struggle, America is the moral force that defeated communism and all those who would put the human soul itself into bondage.

…. A fellow named James Allen once wrote in his diary, "many thinking people believe America has seen its best days." He wrote that July 26, 1775. There are still those who believe America is weakening; that our glory was the brief flash of time called the 20th Century; that ours was a burst of greatness too bright and brilliant to sustain; that America's purpose is past.

My friends, I utterly reject those views. That's not the America we know. We were meant to be masters of destiny, not victims of fate. Who among us would trade America's future for that of any other country in the world? And who could possibly have so little faith in our America that they would trade our tomorrows for our yesterdays?

.... This is the 21st presidential election in my lifetime, the 16th in which I will cast a ballot. Each of those elections had its shifting moods of the moment, its headlines of one day that were forgotten the next. There have been a few more twists and turns this year than in others, a little more shouting about who was up or down, in or out, as we went about selecting our candidates. But now we have arrived, as we always do, at the moment of truth—the serious business of selecting a president. Now is the time for choosing.

As it did 12 years ago, and as we have seen many times in history, our country now stands at a crossroads. There is widespread doubt about our public institutions and profound concern, not merely about the economy but about the overall direction of this great country.

And as they did then, the American people are clamoring for change and sweeping reform. The question we had to ask 12 years ago is the question we ask today: What kind of change can we Republicans offer the American people?

Some might believe that the things we have talked about tonight are irrelevant to the choice. These new isolationists claim that the American people don't care about how or why we prevailed in the great defining struggle of our age—the victory of liberty over our adversaries. They insist that our triumph is yesterday's news, part of a past that holds no lessons for the future.

Well nothing could be more tragic, after having come all this way on the journey of renewal we began 12 years ago, than if America herself forgot the lessons of individual liberty that she has taught to a grateful world.

Emerson was right. We are the country of tomorrow. Our revolution did not end at Yorktown. More than two centuries later, America remains on a voyage of discovery, a land that has never become, but is always in the act of becoming.

But just as we have led the crusade for democracy beyond our shores, we have a great task to do together in our own home. Now, I would appeal to you to invigorate democracy in your own neighborhoods.

Whether we come from poverty or wealth; whether we are Afro-American or Irish-American; Christian or Jewish, from big cities or small towns, we are all equal in the eyes of God. But as Americans that is not enough—we must be equal in the eyes of each other. We can no longer judge each other on the basis of what we are, but must, instead, start finding out who we are. In America, our origins matter less than our destinations and that is what democracy is all about.

A decade after we summoned America to a new beginning, we are beginning still. Every day brings fresh challenges and opportunities to match. With each sunrise we are reminded that millions of our citizens have yet to share in the abundance of American prosperity. Many languish in neighborhoods riddled with drugs and bereft of hope. Still others hesitate to venture out on the streets for fear of criminal violence. Let us pledge ourselves to a new beginning for them.

Let us apply our ingenuity and remarkable spirit to revolutionize education in America so that everyone among us will have the mental tools to build a better life. And while we do so, let's remember that the most profound education begins in the home.

And let us harness the competitive energy that built America, into rebuilding our inner cities so that real jobs can be created for those who live there and real hope can rise out of despair.

Let us strengthen our health care system so that Americans of all ages can be secure in their futures without the fear of financial ruin....

And let us all renew our commitment. Renew our pledge to day by day, person by person, make our country and the world a better place to live. Then when the nations of the world turn to us and say, "America, you are the model of freedom and prosperity." We can turn to them and say, "you ain't seen nothing, yet!"

For me, tonight is the latest chapter in a story that began a quarter of a century ago, when the people of California entrusted me with the stewardship of their dreams.

My fellow citizens—those of you here in this hall and those of you at home—I want you to know that I have always had the highest respect for you, for your common sense and intelligence and for your decency. I have always believed in you and in what you could accomplish for yourselves and for others.

And whatever else history may say about me when I'm gone, I hope it will record that I appealed to your best hopes, not your worst fears, to your confidence rather than your doubts. My dream is that you will travel the road ahead with liberty's lamp guiding your steps and opportunity's arm steadying your way.

My fondest hope for each one of you—and especially for the young people here—is that you will love your country, not for her power or wealth, but for her selflessness and her idealism. May each of you have the heart to conceive, the understanding to direct, and the hand to execute works that will make the world a little better for your having been here.

May all of you as Americans never forget your heroic origins, never fail to seek divine guidance, and never lose your natural, God-given optimism.

And finally, my fellow Americans, may every dawn be a great new beginning for America and every evening bring us closer to that shining city upon a hill.

Before I go, I would like to ask the person who has made my life's journey so meaningful, someone I have been so proud of through the years, to join me. Nancy….

My fellow Americans, on behalf of both of us, goodbye, and God bless each and every one of you, and God bless this country we love.

The Long Goodbye
November 4, 1994

With the publication of this letter, President Reagan informed the nation that he had been diagnosed with Alzheimer's Disease.

My Fellow Americans,

I have recently been told that I am one of the millions of Americans who will be afflicted with Alzheimer's Disease.

Upon learning this news, Nancy and I had to decide whether as private citizens we would keep this a private matter or whether we would make this news known in a public way. In the past Nancy suffered from breast cancer and I had my cancer surgeries. We found through our open disclosures we were able to raise public awareness. We were happy that as a result many more people underwent testing. They were treated in early stages and able to return to normal, healthy lives.

So now, we feel it is important to share it with you. In opening our hearts, we hope this might promote greater awareness of this condition. Perhaps it will encourage a clearer understanding of the individuals and families who are affected by it.

At the moment I feel just fine. I intend to live the remainder of the years God gives me on this earth doing the things I have always done. I will continue to share life's journey with my beloved Nancy and my family. I plan to enjoy the great outdoors and stay in touch with my friends and supporters.

Unfortunately, as Alzheimer's Disease progresses, the family often bears a heavy burden. I only wish there was some way I could spare Nancy from this painful experience. When the time comes I am confident that with your help she will face it with faith and courage.

In closing let me thank you, the American people for giving me the great honor of allowing me to serve as your

President. When the Lord calls me home, whenever that may be, I will leave with the greatest love for this country of ours and eternal optimism for its future. I now begin the journey that will lead me into the sunset of my life. I know that for America there will always be a bright dawn ahead. Thank you, my friends. May God always bless you.

Sincerely,

Ronald Reagan

Bibliography

Cannon, Lou. *Governor Reagan: His Rise To Power.* New York, NY: Public Affairs, 2003.

__________. *President Reagan: The Role Of A Lifetime.* New York, NY: Simon & Schuster, 1991.

__________. *Reagan.* New York, NY: Putnam, 1982.

Carter, Hodding. *The Reagan Years.* New York, NY: Braziller, 1988.

Dallek, Robert. *Ronald Reagan: The Politics of Symbolism.* Cambridge, MA: Harvard University Press, 1984.

Davis, Patti. *Angels Don't Die: My Father's Gift Of Faith.* New York, NY: Harper Collins, 1995.

Deaver, Michael. *Behind The Scenes.* New York, NY: Morrow, 1987.

Edwards, Anne. *Early Reagan.* New York, NY: Morrow, 1987.

Johnson, Haynes. *Sleepwalking Through History: America In The Reagan Years.* New York, NY: Anchor Books, 1992.

Meese III, Edwin. *With Reagan: The Inside Story.* Washington, DC: Regnery Gateway, 1992.

Morris, Edmund. *Dutch: A Memoir Of Ronald Reagan.* New York, NY: Random House, 1999.

Noonan, Peggy. *What I Saw At The Revolution: A Political Life In The Reagan Era.* Boston, MA: G.K. Hall, 1990.

__________. *When Character Was King: A Story of Ronald Reagan.* New York, NY: Viking, 2001.

Reagan, Maureen. *First Father, First Daughter: A Memoir.* New York, NY: Little, Brown & Company, 1989.

Reagan, Nancy. *My Turn: The Memoirs Of Nancy Reagan.* New York, NY: Random House, 1989.

__________. *Nancy.* New York, NY: Morrow, 1980.

Reagan, Ronald. *Reagan: A Life In Letters.* New York, NY: Free Press, 2003.

__________. *A Shining City: The Legacy of Ronald Reagan.* New York, NY: Simon & Schuster, 1998.

__________. *An American Life.* New York, NY: Simon & Schuster, 1990.

__________. *I Love You, Ronnie: The Letters Of Ronald Reagan To Nancy Reagan.* New York, NY: Random House, 2000.

__________. *Stories In His Own Hand: The Everyday Wisdom Of Ronald Reagan.* New York, NY: Free Press, 2001.

__________. *Where's The Rest Of Me?* New York, NY: Duell, Sloan and Pearce, 1985.

Reeves, Richard. *The Reagan Detour.* New York, NY: Simon & Schuster, 1985.

Sick, Gary. *October Surprise: America's Hostages In Iran And The Election Of Ronald Reagan.* New York, NY: Times Books/Random House, 1991.

Speakes, Larry. *Speaking Out: The Reagan Presidency From Inside The White House.* New York, NY: Scribner, 1988.

Wills, Garry. *Reagan's America.* New York, NY: Penguin Books, 1988.